THE ISLE OF MAN

Trevor Kneale

Pevensey Island Guides

FOR GILLIAN

The Pevensey Press is an imprint of
David & Charles

Copyright:
Text © Trevor Kneale 2001
Photographs © Derek Croucher
unless otherwise acknowledged

First published 2001

Map on page 6 by Ethan Danielson

A catalogue record for this book is
available from the British Library.

ISBN 1 898630 25 9

Page layout by
Les Dominey Design Company
Printed in Hong Kong by
Hong Kong Graphics & Printing Ltd
for David & Charles
Brunel House   Newton Abbot   Devon

**Cumberland
Council**
Libraries, book and more......

– 3 JUL 2023 0 4 SEP 2023 13 SEP " 24 - 4 - 24 0 7 SEP 2024 0 7 SEP 2024		

Please return/renew this item by the last date due.
Library items may also be renewed by phone on
030 33 33 1234 (24hours) or via our website

www.cumberland.gov.uk/libraries-and-archives

CONTENTS

Page 1: Isle of Man steam railway
Pages 2-3: Cashtal-yn-Ard
Left: Sunset from the Ayres

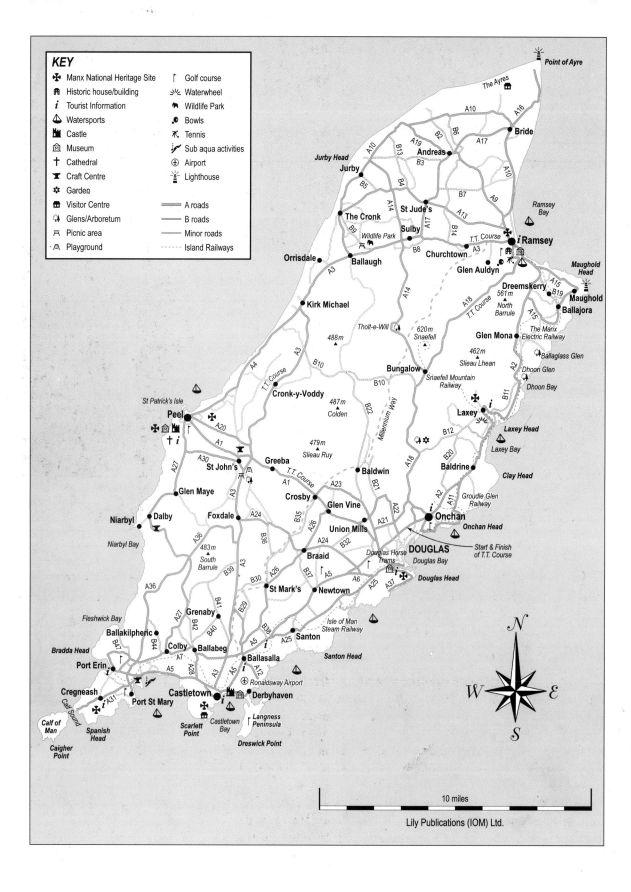

KEY

- Manx National Heritage Site
- Historic house/building
- *i* Tourist Information
- Watersports
- Castle
- Museum
- Cathedral
- Craft Centre
- Garden
- Visitor Centre
- Glens/Arboretum
- Picnic area
- Playground

- Golf course
- Waterwheel
- Wildlife Park
- Bowls
- Tennis
- Sub aqua activities
- Airport
- Lighthouse
- A roads
- B roads
- Minor roads
- Island Railways

Point of Ayre

The Ayres

Jurby Head

Bride

A10 A16 A17

Jurby

Andreas

A10 A19 B2 B6

B13 B3

St Jude's

B5 B4 A14 A17 B7 A9 A13

Ramsey Bay

The Cronk

Sulby

B9 B8 A3

Churchtown

T.T. Course

Ramsey

Orrisdale

Ballaugh

A3

Glen Auldyn

Maughold Head

Dreemskerry

561 m North Barrule

A15 B19

Maughold

Ballajora

Kirk Michael

A3 A14 A18 T.T. Course

Glen Mona

The Manx Electric Railway

Tholt-e-Will

488 m

620 m Snaefell

A4 A3 B10

Bungalow

462 m Slieau Lhean

Ballaglass Glen

Dhoon Glen

Dhoon Bay

St Patrick's Isle

Cronk-y-Voddy

B10

Snaefell Mountain Railway

A2 B11

Peel

487 m Colden

B22

Laxey

Laxey Head

A20

479 m Slieau Ruy

Millennium Way

Laxey Bay

A1

Greeba

St John's

A30 A1

T.T. Course

Baldwin

B12

Baldrine

Clay Head

Glen Maye

A27 A3

Crosby

A23

B21 A18 B20

Dalby

Foxdale

A24

Glen Vine

B35

Union Mills

A22 Onchan Onchan Head

Niarbyl

A36 483 m South Barrule

B36 B26 A24 B32

A21

DOUGLAS

Groudle Glen Railway

A11

Niarbyl Bay

Braid

Douglas Horse Trams

Start & Finish of T.T. Course

A36

B39 B30 A26 B37 A5

St Mark's

Newtown

A6 A25 A37

Douglas Bay

Douglas Head

Fleshwick Bay

Grenaby

B41 B42 B40 B29 B38

Isle of Man Steam Railway

Bradda Head

Ballakilpheric

Colby Ballabeg

A5 A25 Santon

Santon Head

Port Erin

B47 A7 A28 A3 A5 A12

Ballasalla

Ronaldsway Airport

Cregneash

A31

Port St Mary

Castletown Derbyhaven

Langness Peninsula

Calf Sound

Scarlett Point

Castletown Bay

Calf of Man

Spanish Head

Dreswick Point

Caigher Point

N
W   E
S

10 miles

Lily Publications (IOM) Ltd.

1 AN INDEPENDENT NATION

Above: Sulby Glen in late autumn

THE MOTTO WHICH APPEARS with the official Three Legs of Man emblem is an appropriate comment on the resilience of the Isle of Man: *Quocunque Jeceris Stabit* ('It will stand wheresoever you throw it'). The Manx have survived a roller-coaster ride through history and have never been more prosperous or independent than they are today.

A self-governing Crown dependency, the Isle of Man does not belong to the United Kingdom or Great Britain but is part of the British Isles and the Commonwealth of Nations. It has its own parliament, administrative system and laws but pays Britain to take responsibility for international affairs and defence, with Her Majesty the Queen retaining the title Lord of Mann. Relations with the EU are limited to trade and do not extend to financial aid.

There are reminders everywhere of a potent heritage stretching back to Neolithic times and especially of those centuries when the Kingdom of Mann & the Isles was a strategic pawn fought over by Norse, Scots and

COAT OF ARMS

Augmented version of the Coat of Arms of the Isle of Man, granted by Royal Warrant in 1996. The three legs device seems to have been adopted in the thirteenth century as the armorial bearings of the ancient Kings of the Isle of Man, whose dominion included the Hebrides. The motto which has been associated with the Island since about 1300 translates 'withersoever you throw it, it will stand'. Supporters assigned to the Arms are the Peregrine Falcon, alluding to a tradition (begun in 1405) of giving two falcons to each King of England on his coronation day, and the Raven, a bird of legend and superstition rooted in Norse history.

Above: Port Erin

Right: Garwick Bay – once a smuggler's haunt

English kings. Situated in the middle of the Irish Sea, the Island was a welcome landfall for prehistoric, Celtic and Norse migrants and an ideal base for Viking rulers eager to plunder the neighbouring coastlines of England, Scotland, Ireland and Wales. To the Manx, the Isle of Man is the mainland and the surrounding countries are the adjacent isles 'across the water'.

Located roughly equidistant from those other countries, the Island measures 33 x 13 miles (52 x 22km) and has a total land area of 221 square miles (572 sq km) of which more than 40 per cent is uninhabited. The population is 74,000 and rising with almost half living in the Douglas/ Onchan/Braddan area. For administrative and political purposes, the Isle of Man is divided into six ancient sheadings (Gaelic *seden*, ie six), each of which elects representatives to the Manx parliament. There are seventeen ecclesiastical parishes named after patron saints, some of them quite obscure. The six sheadings with their parishes in brackets are: Ayre (Bride, Andreas and Lezayre); Michael (Michael, Ballaugh and Jurby); Glenfaba (Patrick and German); Garff (Onchan, Maughold and Lonan); Middle (Marown, Braddan and Santon); Rushen (Rushen, Arbory and Malew).

POST-WAR PROSPERITY

The Manx are proud of their parliament, history, folklore, customs and language (although few today can speak it). They issue their own postage stamps and currency but English and Scottish money is welcome. Tourism has contributed to the Manx exchequer ever since Victorian holidaymakers began to arrive in shiploads. The battalions who came mainly for sea-and-sand holidays have long since departed for the Costas leaving today's discerning visitors to enjoy the wide open spaces and an exceptional choice of activities. The 350,000 who come each year have never been better catered for although tourism, like the old industries of fishing, crofting and mining, is no longer a major source of revenue.

The burgeoning financial-services sector is the big earner and the Isle

THE MANX HOLLYWOOD

Most visible among many new service industries is film making. Thanks to initiatives launched by the IoM Film Commission and the lure of the scenery, a host of stars – David Bowie, Patrick Bergen, John Hurt, Kate Beckinsale, Kathleen Turner, John Gordon Sinclair and Sir Peter Ustinov, among others – have been seen filming in the 'Manx Hollywood'. Several TV series and numerous feature films have been made on the island: the comedy Waking Ned, *supposedly set in Ireland, was shot entirely in Manx locations.*

HM THE QUEEN ON TYNWALD HILL

In 1979, Tynwald's millennium year, HM The Queen took the central seat on Tynwald Hill, once occupied by Norse kings. The sovereign's representative, the lieutenant-governor, presides over the annual ceremony but, since 1990, his duties in the Tynwald Court in Douglas have been undertaken by a president elected by the members of Tynwald. Also present are the Lord Bishop, the two deemsters (or judges), the Legislative Council (formerly the Lord of Man's principal officers), members of the Keys, and clergy and captains of parishes. Freemen or commoners gather on the outside of the central mound.

of Man has become an important player on the international investment scene. More than 42,000 companies are registered in the Island. There has been a prosperous knock-on effect and less than 2 per cent of the economically active population is unemployed with five vacancies on offer for every person out of work.

The Manx government is responsible for all revenue and expenditure. Basic income tax is set at 15 per cent rising to a maximum of 20 per cent, paid by about a quarter of tax payers – there is no capital-gains tax or inheritance tax. Given these incentives and the quality of life on the Island it is not surprising that there has been an influx of new residents, including the rich and famous. Some come to take advantage of job opportunities, others to enjoy either tranquil or active retirement in a clean, green environment. Native Manx people enjoy certain privileges in employment and council housing matters but numbers have fallen to less than half the population. Inevitably, most young people feel the need to travel and gain experience but as the Island prospers increasing numbers are returning home.

In common with other people of Celtic origin, the Manx have proved to be hardy emigrants and you will find them all over the world. Cleveland, Ohio, for example, was populated by Manx settlers, and other links date back to the Pilgrim Fathers. A World Manx Congress meets regularly and there are branches of the Manx Society in the USA, Australia, New Zealand, South Africa and England. Manx emigrants and their descendants take part in homecomings at regular intervals, perhaps remembering the Manx national anthem:

O land of our birth, O Gem of God's earth
O Island so strong and so fair, Built firm as Barrule
Thy throne of Home Rule, Makes us free as thy sweet mountain air.

AN ANCIENT PARLIAMENT

Tynwald (Norse *thingvollr* – assembly field or meeting place) is the oldest parliament in continuous existence in the world. Some historians believe it be much older than its millennium celebrated in 1979; Vikings were in effective occupation by the end of the ninth century when assemblies of freemen were already an essential part of Norse life. The Manx parliament comprises twenty-four members of a popularly elected lower chamber (the House of Keys) and an upper house, the Legislative Council, consisting of three *ex-officio* members – the President of Tynwald, the Lord Bishop of Sodor & Man (Sodor refers to the medieval diocese which included the Hebrides: the Sudreys, or Southern Isles) and the attorney general – and eight members elected by the House of Keys. They sit in separate chambers in Douglas and come together to agree new legislation in a combined body known as the Tynwald Court. In early July each year there is an open-air

assembly in St John's on Tynwald Hill, a modest mound which was the site of national gatherings before the coming of the Norsemen. Following a church service, dignitaries and officers, some in traditional robes, process behind the thirteenth-century Manx Sword of State to the hill, and there new laws are proclaimed in English and Manx.

There has been much speculation over the origin of the name Keys. The Manx name has long been *Yn Kiare-es-Feed* – 'the four and twenty'. When the earliest English officials arrived in the island they may have taken *kiare-es* to mean 'keys' which also tied in with the notion of the parliament 'unlocking' the Laws. The modern Speaker of the House of Keys has duties which go beyond those of his Westminster counterpart. In addition to keeping order he is the spokesman of the House and attends Tynwald as an elected member. A closer comparison with the UK is the appointment of a chief minister and a council of ministers responsible for various government departments.

Tynwald Day, when the world's oldest continuous parliament is celebrated in style. After the pageantry and proclamations everyone can join in the fun of the Tynwald Fair (IoM Tourism)

THE MANX CHARACTER

Manx people are known to be generally good-natured, although often careful and reserved. They manage to combine elements of the relaxing *traa-dy-liooar* ('time enough') philosophy with a remarkable degree of resilience and enterprise. In the past they resisted the hardships inflicted by church and state and were not slow to protest against excessive tithes or unjust land enclosures. The Manx have always cherished their ancient

Votes for Women

The Manx have made a significant contribution to the promotion of women's rights. In 1881, the Isle of Man was the first country in the world to introduce votes for women (New Zealand was the second). Initially, the franchise was restricted to owners of real estate valued at £4 or more, but by 1919 all women in the Island were enfranchised, nine years ahead of their UK counterparts. Emmeline Pankhurst (1857-1928), heroic leader of the campaign for women's rights in the UK, was the daughter of a Manx woman: Sophia Jane Craine, who was born at Lonan in 1835 and married Robert Goulden at Kirk Braddan in 1853. Emmeline was born in Manchester but she spent part of her childhood in the Isle of Man and was a frequent visitor.

Above: Laxey Great Wheel

Right: Gravestones and wild garlic – Old Kirk Braddan

rights and having had their own parliament for more than a thousand years, they have not experienced the devolutionary agonies suffered by the Scots, Irish and Welsh. Their desire to be heard extends into local government: Douglas has been a municipal borough since 1896; Ramsey, Castletown, Peel and several village districts have their own commissioners, and even parishes have a voice. All these authorities have contributed to the development of the Island's exceptional public services and amenities. Law and order in this largely peaceable island is another issue which is taken very seriously. The Isle of Man Constabulary (there is 1 police officer for every 344 residents) is popular with everyone, except proven offenders!

Mysterious Origins

The precise origin of the Island's name is not known but it probably derives from a pre-Celtic root meaning 'mountainous or hilly land'. In 54BC Julius Caesar called it *Mona*; Scandinavian sagas use *Mon* or *Maon*; and it is *Manaw* in Welsh annals. Romantics suggest that Mann was named after Manannan Mac Lir, a Celtic hero, but this is unlikely. Legend also has it that before the coming of Christianity the island was the haunt of Manannan Mac Lir, a necromancer who kept strangers away by magically covering the land with mist. Those who dared to approach were faced with a hundred phantom men ready to repel invaders.

Use of a three-legs motif can be traced back to the Greeks in the sixth century BC. Like the ancient swastika or fylfot the design is derived from the spokes of a wheel, in turn representing rays of the sun. There is evidence that the Three Legs of Man emblem (*Trje Cassyn*) was used by Vikings in the ninth century AD before being replaced by a ship emblem. It may have been reintroduced in 1266 by Alexander III of Scotland in deference to the Three Legs of Sicily where he had family connections. The earliest-known reproduction on the island appears on the Manx Sword of State and the fourteenth-century Maughold Cross. Controversy over the way in which the emblem should be depicted was finally settled in the 1950s when researchers drew attention to eighteenth-century Manx coins with the legs running the wrong way (anticlockwise). Worse, this error was perpetuated into the next century on letterheads, badges, souvenirs and, most unfortunate of all, prominent buildings including the great Laxey Wheel of 1854!

Language Revival

A general resurgence of interest in Gaelic languages has produced a growing number of Manx speakers of all ages, and Manx Gaelic is an optional subject in schools up to GCSE level. In the mid eighteenth century, most of the population spoke only Manx (strictly speaking 'Manks' – there is no X

PROMOTING MANX HERITAGE

The Isle of Man has one of the most concentrated and best-cared-for historic landscapes in Europe and the celebration of its treasures is a part of Manx life in which visitors are encouraged to share. Much credit is due to Manx National Heritage, a dedicated professional body funded largely by the Manx Government.

Unique in Europe for a range of achievements, this organisation has been studied by more than a dozen other countries and has won numerous British and international awards. Manx national history may be studied at graduate and post-graduate level at the Centre for Manx Studies created in partnership with the Island's Department of Education and Liverpool University. Manx National Heritage manages ten museum sites, preserves ancient monuments throughout the landscape, controls all archaeological investigations and protects areas of outstanding natural beauty and ecological significance.

Above: Thatched roof, Cregneash

Right: Yn Cruinnaght Inter-Celtic Festival, Ramsey (IoM Tourism)

in the Gaelic) but a hundred years on, the majority spoke only English. Numerous Manx words and expressions survive in everyday conversation, and the language is celebrated at the *Yn Chruinnaght* festivals and in many other ways, underlining a growing interest in Manx literature, music and dance. Place names throughout the Island are reminders of the mother tongue and there are signposts written in both Manx and English.

Some older people retain the distinctive and musical Manx accent which so delighted T.E. Brown (1830-97), the Manx national poet. Born in Douglas, the younger son of the Vicar of Braddan, Brown was a brilliant academic who retained a lifelong love for the Island and its people. Many of his best poems are in the Manx dialect but his wider reputation rests on verse which celebrates nature – 'The Blackbird' and 'My Garden' for example. If he were around today, Brown would approve of the manner in which Manx culture is being preserved and promoted by a number of dedicated bodies including the government-funded Manx National Heritage and the Manx Heritage Foundation which supports the performing and visual arts, Manx-language studies, academic research projects and publications.

Manx, Scottish and Irish Gaelic belong to the Goidelic branch of the ancient Celtic language whose speakers followed direct sea routes from western France and bypassed Britain. There was Gaelic speech in the Isle of Man from at least the fifth century AD. Brythonic Gaelic, which includes Welsh, Cornish and Breton, entered south-east England from the continent in pre-Roman days.

During the years of Viking conquest, Manx Gaelic was challenged by the Norse language but after the Scots took over in 1266 it again became the chief speech of the Manx people. Few traces of Norse remain in the language (as opposed to profound influences in law making and administration) except in place names and, even here, Celtic names outnumber Norse by six to one.

WISE WORDS AND FAIRY TALES

Traditional Manx proverbs are full of sentiment, wit and wisdom. Examples, in translation from the Manx, include: 'There are many twists in the marriage tune'/'A man has his own will, but a woman has her own way'/'A gossip's mouth is the devil's postbag'/'Maybe the last dog is catching the hare'/'They that sow seeds of kindness will reap harvests of love'/'Don't tell me what I was but tell me what I am'/'Don't marry an heiress unless her father has been hanged.'

Manx people have the Celtic gift of imaginative story-telling. Their folklore records the exploits of numerous witches, elves, hobgoblins and other, largely malevolent supernatural beings including the gigantic, big-voiced Buggane and the ugly, beast-like Phynnodderee. Old customs and superstitions, such as putting out food and drink 'for the fairies' persisted into the twentieth century.

2 THE VARIED NATURE OF MAN

THE SEVEN KINGDOMS OF SNAEFELL

On the often-misty summit of Snaefell mountain there is a restaurant and from the viewing platforms the Manx say you can see seven kingdoms – England, Scotland, Ireland, Wales, Man, the Kingdom of the Sea and the Kingdom of Heaven.

ISOLATION, TOPOGRAPHY, CLIMATE and the activities of its inhabitants since pre-history have shaped the Island's landscape, habitats and species. Wildlife flourishes in an exceptional concentration of terrestrial and marine environments – a mountainous interior, traditional farmland, wooded glens, wild moorland, massive cliffs, shingle beaches, wetland areas and the surrounding sea.

An equable climate explains why tender wildflowers and semi-exotic shrubs thrive out of doors. The ubiquitous Gulf Stream washes and warms the Isle of Man before travelling on to create other pleasant, if diminishing, micro-climates on the west coast of Scotland – the Rhins of Galloway and Plockton, near Skye, for example. Extreme variations of temperature are not shared with other places on the same degree of latitude (eg Yorkshire), and the mean winter temperature is higher than in all counties on the south coast of England, excepting parts of Cornwall. Snow is rare and frost infrequent. Prevailing winds are generally mild but exposed places can be wind-blown, especially in winter. By British standards, the Island enjoys above-average sunshine although the higher summer temperatures may be tempered by a breeze.

SPECTACULAR ROCK FORMATIONS

Geology is not everyone's first passion but visitors often reach for their cameras when they see the Island's rock formations. Geologists have been studying what is known as the Manx Group of rocks for many years. These are the hard slates and grits, formed from sediments deposited some 500 million years ago, which make up the central highland mass and give rise to rocky cliffs around the coast. Frequent earth movements have twisted the rocks from the horizontal into spectacular shapes, leaving miles of striking coastal scenery. Those who know their rocks may spot granite at Foxdale and Dhoon, limestone near Castletown and red sandstone surrounding Peel.

The impressive hills which form the Island's backbone are known as 'the mountains' although only Snaefell ('snow mountain') at 2,036ft (621m) meets the official height requirement. The quickest and most memorable way to the top of this much-visited peak is by vintage mountain railway which starts down at Laxey on the coast and climbs up through a broad, green glen.

This central land mass consists of a moorland plateau around 750ft (229m) high, above which rise a number of peaks, most over 1,500ft (457m). A dominant line of hills extends north-east to south-west from North Barrule, near Ramsey, through Snaefell, Beinn y Phott, Carraghan, Colden and Greeba. Most of these hills can be reached from the Millennium Way footpath created in 1979 to mark a thousand years of Tynwald. Below the uplands is a lower plateau 300-600ft (91-183m) high, and two main lowland areas – one north of Ramsey, the other a smaller expanse near Castletown, both created by glacial drift.

A UNIQUE ECOLOGY

Naturalists have studied and continue to monitor every aspect of Manx wildlife from vast bird colonies to shy basking sharks, from rare orchids to polecats. Isolation has resulted in the exclusion of a number of species native to other parts of the British Isles such as woodpeckers, badgers, newts and snakes, but there are more gains than losses.

Information on where to go and what to see is available from Manx Tourism and Leisure, the Manx Wildlife Trust (MWT) – which has 20

AN IRISH ELK IN MAN

Irish Elk (Megaloceras giganteus) were among the last living creatures to reach the Isle of Man by land-bridge from present-day Cumbria. Remains of these giant deer – they were not a true elk – have been found in the island and a magnificent specimen, with antlers 10ft (3m) wide, can be seen in the Manx Museum. The Isle of Man became an island about 9,000 years ago and went on to develop an ecology of its own.

Opposite: Primroses and wood anenomes in Dhoon Glen

17

nature reserves covering 234 acres (95ha) – and Manx National Heritage (MNH), responsible for the Calf of Man and other areas of outstanding natural beauty and ecological significance. Birdwatchers may wish to contact Manx Bird Atlas (MBA), an organisation which conducts a continuous research programme to establish the breeding and wintering populations of birds in the Isle of Man. Every 1km square on the Island is being surveyed to determine the distribution and abundance of each breeding species. MBA researchers work closely with the government which uses the data to help shape official conservation policy. Another contributor to the knowledge of bird life is the Manx Ornithological Society which publishes an annual bird report. Contact telephone numbers for all these organisations can be found in the Further Information section at the end of this book.

THE CALF OF MAN BIRD SANCTUARY

There is insufficient space here to highlight all of the many exceptional wildlife locations in the Isle of Man but the Calf of Man, a 616-acre (250ha) islet off the south-western tip, is a good starting point. A visit to the Calf combines a lively boat trip with an opportunity to observe a colony of grey seals which breed on the undisturbed rocky coastline. In summer, regular sailings operate from Port Erin and, occasionally, from Port St Mary. Those using their own boats are advised to take local advice before attempting to negotiate the swirling tidal flow of the Calf Sound. Precipitous cliffs and the dangerous waters limit the safe landing places to South Harbour, a small

Above: Manx Shearwater emerging from its burrow (Manx Bird Atlas)
Right: Sunset over the Calf of Man

BIRDS ON THE CALF

An official bird observatory was opened at the Calf of Man in 1962 and since that time more than 100,000 birds have been ringed and 260 species recorded. A wide variety of resident and migrant species is monitored from March to November each year. Wardens live in the observatory (once the main farmhouse) where there is also dormitory accommodation for visiting ornithologists and birdwatchers.

Below: Chough are resident breeders (Manx Bird Atlas)

Below right: Loaghtan sheep – a Manx breed – are rare, but their numbers are on the increase

inlet, Cow Harbour and Grant's Harbour, little more than a cleft in the rock.

Difficulty of access has curtailed the extent of human habitation on the Calf although there is evidence for an ancient Celtic keeill and a long history of crofting. During the English Civil War, the Earl of Derby fortified the islet and charged the occupier a rental of 500 'puffins', actually Manx shearwater. These birds (first named on the Calf in 1676) were once harvested as food and their oil used both to condition wool and to clean firearms.

After many years of agricultural and holiday use, the Calf of Man passed from private ownership into the hands of the English National Trust and then to the Manx National Trust. Today, the Calf is a bird sanctuary of international importance.

Huge colonies of guillemot, kittiwake, fulmar and other seabirds nest on the slate cliffs or take advantage of a large expanse of rough pasture and heather. The acrobatic chough, a red-legged member of the crow family, breeds more densely on the Calf than anywhere else, and like raven, water rail and stonechat, is a permanent resident. Storm petrel, eider, skua, hen harrier and short-eared owl are seen and some of the rarities on record confirm that this is a 'twitcher's' paradise: osprey, red kite, goshawk, bluethroat, pechora pipit, aquatic warbler, woodchat, shrike, sabine's gull, red-breasted flycatcher and scarlet rosefinch.

The Calf is also home to a flock of rare Loaghtan sheep, a native Manx breed whose brown wool (*loaghtan* means mousey brown) was the staple of Manx clothing for centuries. These splendid four-horned animals were in danger of extinction but roam freely now in their secure Island home.

OTHER SEABIRD COLONIES

Hen harrier and young
(Manx Bird Atlas)

Other breeding sites on the Manx mainland at Peel Hill, Maughold Head, the Chasms and Sugarloaf rock, underline the Island's importance as a southerly extension of major seabird colonies on the west side of Britain. Gulls and fulmars have colonies all round the rocky coastline while kittiwake, guillemot and razorbill favour the awesome Chasms and the 100ft (30m) Sugarloaf, a detached rock, between Port St Mary and the Calf Sound. The Chasms consist of a series of deep fissures extending inland for about 246ft (75m) from sheer, perpendicular cliffs. There is a car park reached by a lane south of Cregneash but from there you descend on foot, taking great care to avoid crevices half-concealed by furze and heather. Nearby is the Sugarloaf, named for its shape, and a number of caves which can be explored by boat.

Continuing round the bay towards the Calf of Man, the cliffs rise to 400ft (122m) above the sea at Spanish Head where a ship from the fleeing Spanish Armada is said to have foundered. There are more colonies of

seabirds and this is also a nesting habitat for raven, chough and peregrine falcon. MNH manages 200 acres (81ha) of the unspoiled coastline plus the Calf Sound, Kitterland (a rocky islet), the Chasms and a large area of publicly accessible countryside which takes in Cregneash Folk Village and Meayl Hill. A great variety of birds can be seen at Scarlett, near Castletown, where there is a visitor centre and nature trail managed by MWT. Some of the rock formations are extraordinary and from the nature trail it is possible to see almost the entire chain of Manx mountains.

Langness peninsula, near Castletown and the airport, is an excellent area for watching waders and wildfowl. There are some lovely wildflowers – spring squill, dodder, common milkvetch and field gentian – but Langness's main claim to ecological fame is the lesser-mottled grasshopper (*Stenobothrus stigmaticus*), not found elsewhere in the British Isles.

A WILDLIFE WONDERLAND

Ballaugh Curragh, a peaceful expanse of wetland in the north, is teeming with wildlife – not least six species of orchid and western Europe's largest winter roost of hen harrier, an uncommon visitor elsewhere. The Curragh (Manx for willow carr) consists of marshy grassland dotted with willow and bog myrtle, open water, birch woodland and flower-rich hayfields. This unique woodland and wetland occupies the basin of an Ice Age lake which has been drying out slowly ever since. Marshy ground is difficult to farm but worked flints found here indicate the presence of man from Neolithic times. For centuries the area was used for early grazing and peat digging; trees were coppiced for basketmaking and rushes cut for thatch. The first recorded attempt to improve drainage occurred in 1648 when the Lhen Trench was dug out. As a result some land was reclaimed, becoming hay meadows which provided valuable animal fodder. With the arrival of heavy farm machinery unsuited to the boggy terrain the Curragh was largely abandoned until its environmental value was recognised.

Today, most of this landscape is carefully managed by MNH and MWT whose brief is to conserve and improve the many wildlife habitats. The Curragh also encompasses Close Sartfield, a 31-acre (13ha) nature reserve owned by MWT. From late May to early July, tens of thousands of orchids (some rare) bloom in the hay meadows together with yellow bartsia, yellow rattle, purple loosestrife and cuckoo flower. In peaty areas bog myrtle and purple moor grass predominate while bogbean, marsh cinquefoil, devil's bit scabious, cotton grass and many other plants proliferate in wet locations. The stately royal fern (the largest in these islands) turns a striking orange colour in autumn. Butterflies, moths, damselflies and dragonflies are common and the Curragh is home to brown hare, rabbit, woodmice, pygmy shrew, stoat, polecat-ferret, frogs, lizards and bats.

Opposite: The Chasms, near Spanish Head

Below: Wild orchids flourish (Manx Wildlife Trust)

THE CURRAGHS WILDLIFE PARK

At the Curraghs Wildlife Park, where more than 100 birds and animals have been gathered from all over the world, a series of walk-through exhibits recreates the endangered Amazon forest, an Asian swamp, a European marsh, a North American trail, the African bush and the South American pampas. Each animal or bird lives in an environment as close as possible to the native wild: scarlet macaws, green and spider monkeys, red deer, black swans, lynx, antelope, emu, flamingo, otters, wallabies, mongoose, tapirs, owls, chipmunks and many more. There are butterfly and nature trails to follow and a miniature steam railway which operates in the summer.

Above: Pelican in the park
Right: Sea holly; birdsfoot trefoil (Manx Wildlife Trust)
Opposite above: Point of Ayre Lighthouse
Opposite below: A massive shark – but harmless (Ken Watterson, Basking Shark Society)

There is a highly successful food chain in this environment commencing with thriving invertebrates taken by small birds, in turn sought out by stoats, polecat-ferrets and birds of prey. In addition to the hen harrier, peregrine falcon and merlin can be seen. Breeding species include lesser redpoll, grasshopper warbler, reed bunting, sedge warbler, whitethroat, curlew, water rail and the endangered corncrake which returned to breed in 1999, thanks to good meadow management. Grazed by sheep in winter, the hay meadows are cut in late summer once the wildflowers have seeded. Footpaths wind through the reserve and a specially constructed birdwatching hide – suitable for wheelchairs – is reached by a boardwalk not far from the entrance. The platform of the bird hide allows a panoramic view of the entire area with a backdrop of northern hills. In winter, the sight of hen harriers coming home to roost at dusk is quite unforgettable.

SAND, SHINGLE AND RARE WILDFLOWERS

At the northernmost point of the Isle of Man is an area known as the Ayres, a raised shingle beach of post-glacial origin backed by sand dunes and an extremely rare lichen-dominated heath. The coastline of the Ayres (old Norse *eyrr* meaning 'gravel bank') is continually being changed by material deposits eroded from cliffs to the south. From this breezy vantage point you can look beyond the Point of Ayre lighthouse towards the Galloway coast, only 17 miles (27km) away. Blue-grey sea holly and pink-flowered sea bindweed grow amongst the marram grass and lizards feed on abundant grasshoppers. Isle of Man cabbage, pyramidal orchid, sea and portland spurges thrive in the sea air. The heath is a botanist's delight, thick with mosses, lichens, wild thyme, storksbill, dovesfoot, cranesbill, rest harrow, birdsfoot trefoil and summer-flowering burnet roses. In boggy spots there are orchids, ferns, pennywort, pimpernel and other wildflowers.

A variety of birds is attracted to the Ayres: gannet and cormorant dive for fish, waders feed on the shoreline, seabirds nest on the dunes and heathland where skylark and stonechat also breed. The entire stretch of sand and shingle from the Ayres to Jurby is a rewarding walk for birdwatchers. They will encounter mallard, shelduck, lapwing, curlew, oystercatcher and, in the breeding season, arctic tern and little tern nesting on the beach. Out to sea, basking shark, seal, porpoise and, occasionally, dolphin defy the treacherous *streuss* ('strife') created as tides from each side of the island meet off the point. MWT manages the popular Ayres Visitor Centre and Nature Trail where walkers must use boardwalks and keep dogs on the lead so as not to damage the fragile vegetation or disturb the nesting seabirds.

MANN'S WELCOMING WATERS

In summer, basking shark, the second-largest fish in the world, feeds in the plankton-rich waters which surround the island. This huge creature can grow up to 33ft (10m) in length but is harmless and eats only plankton which it filters through its gaping mouth and gills. The Isle of Man is one of the best watching sites in Europe and trips to see the gentle giants attract visitors from all over the world. Scientists record the habits of these great sharks and experienced divers swim with them. Trips are organised by the Basking Shark Society whose pioneer work under the direction of Ken Watterson has been featured on television and in leading wildlife publications.

In addition to a resident population of grey seal, dolphin and porpoise, orca, mink and pilot whales are often sighted off the Manx coast. Many seabirds feed in local waters: auk, shag, cormorant, Manx shearwater, storm petrel and, largest of all, gannet. Scuba divers enjoy the clear waters where there is an abundance of colourful marine life including anemones, starfish and octopus. MWT's Marine Interpretation Centre at the Port Erin Marine Laboratory is open to the public from March to October.

RESTORING THE WOODLANDS

The clearance of trees for farming and early man's dependency on wood for charcoal and house-building led to a serious loss of woodland in the Isle of Man. The landscape was virtually treeless by the seventeeth century but in the following century bishops and landowners made tree planting a priority. Anyone who cut down a tree without permission was fined and made to plant a replacement. Many mature beech, larch, horse chestnut and pine trees are the fruits of this enlightened policy. Pleasure gardens

THE PORT ERIN MARINE LABORATORY

Marine research began in the Isle of Man in 1892 when Professor (later Sir) William Herdman established a modest laboratory and an aquarium on the south side of Port Erin Bay. This blossomed into a world-renowned marine laboratory under the aegis of Liverpool University's Department of Oceanography. Many outstanding marine biologists have benefited from and contributed to this centre of scientific excellence.

were created by the Victorians who enhanced the delightful Manx National Glens by planting beech, wych elm, ash, oak, sycamore, horse chestnut and sweet chestnut.

Afforestation of the hills began in the 1880s with plantations at Archallagan, South Barrule and Greeba and was most intense between the 1950s and the 1990s. Not all the plantations on the heathland are as attractive as Tholt-y-Will plantation which is largely a mixture of spruce, larch and pine. Efforts are being made to improve the stock of deciduous trees: 6,000 saplings, germinated from acorns by primary-school children from all over the island, were planted in March 2000 to create a 20-acre (8ha) Millennium Oakwood at Ballafletcher, Braddan.

Above & opposite: Soothing images in Dhoon Glen

NATIVE BREEDS

Decimation of the wildwood undoubtedly caused the loss of some animal and plant species. Bones of wild cat and red deer have been excavated and there may have been wolves, foxes, pine marten and red squirrel. The Island had its own hardy breeds of ponies, pigs, cattle, goat and sheep from the Celtic period right up to the nineteenth century when imported breeds took over. As late as 1845, wild pigs ('purrs') were living on South Barrule but were eventually hunted down at Braddan. Feral goats still roam on land at the Dhoon and Bulgham Brooghs ('sandy slopes') on the coast between Laxey and Maughold. Close by are the cliff haunts of chough, raven and peregrine whose habitat has never been threatened.

Below: Cat with no tail to tell! (IoM Tourism)

Native Loaghtan sheep (best seen grazing on the Calf of Man) are preserved as a rare breed by the Loaghtan Sheep Society and there is another animal which is synonymous with the Isle of Man – the tail-less Manx cat. Tail-less cats are known in Asia but few are found in Europe. There is an unproven theory that these loveable creatures arrived in the island from a foreign vessel wrecked off Spanish Head. True Manxies have longer hind legs that those of other cats and have a distinctive action when they move. Entirely tail-less ones are known as 'rumpies' and those with partial tails are 'stumpies'. Owing to inbreeding, Manx cats have become less common although they are kept as pets and make excellent farm cats. There are no prizes for guessing that the most popular name for them is 'Kipper'!

3 FROM STONE AGE TO COMPUTER AGE

THERE IS PROOF OF HUNTER-FISHERMEN living in coastal areas of the Isle of Man well before 5000BC, during the Mesolithic period or Middle Stone Age. A thousand years on, in Neolithic times, a knowledge of land cultivation and animal husbandry arrived via sea trade from the Mediterranean. At that stage, the straits of Dover may not have been navigable and travellers would have sailed around the coasts of Spain, Portugal and France to reach the western side of Britain. Trade routes continued northwards beyond the Isle of Man to Scotland and on to Scandinavia and the Baltic.

Weapons, tools and utensils used by these early settlers have been found throughout the island. Excavations at Ronaldsway in 1943, during work on the airport, revealed a primitive oblong dwelling house about 24 x 14ft (7 x 4m), complete with a hearth near the centre – the earliest known example of a British-type longhouse, where people lived at one end and animals at the other. Considerable quantities of animal bones, pottery and tools were unearthed together with five small, decorated slate plaques hitherto unknown in the British Isles and, possibly, of Mediterranean origin. Traders and migrants must have travelled about the Irish Sea even in those distant, unrecorded days with the Isle of Man at the geographical centre of their activities.

WHEN BRONZE GAVE WAY TO IRON

From around 2000BC to the beginning of the Iron Age in 500BC, bronze (an alloy of copper and tin) was used for making tools, weapons and ornaments to augment the tried-and-trusted stone axeheads and flint knives. The Isle of Man is thought to have been one of the most active bronze-using locations because the necessary materials were on hand or could be shipped in. There was a demand for bronze artefacts for a time

Above and right: The Braaid, Marown – site of a circular Celtic homestead and two later Norse dwellings

OGHAM SCRIPT – EARLY CELTIC RECORDS

Stones inscribed with ogham lettering are proof of the links which existed between different parts of Celtic Britain. This method of writing (letters are formed by a series of marks cut into the stone) was developed in south-west Ireland before spreading to Scotland, Wales, Cornwall and the Isle of Man. Although most inscriptions simply record the name of the person being commemorated, they are the earliest written records of Celtic speech. Ogham-inscribed stones can be seen at Andreas, Rushen and Arbory.

Above: Thorwald's cross-slab, Andreas, incomplete but an outstanding example from the Norse period

Opposite: 'Odin's Raven' – replica Viking ship brought to life in the House of Manannan, Peel

but, gradually, all forms of trade diminished along the Atlantic seaways. By 100BC, Celts with ironworking skills had reached the Island to begin a new era of economic and cultural development.

During the long Celtic Iron Age, agricultural and stock-raising methods improved and people took to spinning, weaving, pottery and jewellery-making. Huge roundhouses, up to 90ft (27m) in diameter, were centres of social power occupied by chieftains and their followers. Lesser folk lived in smaller roundhouses, some fortified, and their livelihood came mainly from breeding cattle, horses, sheep, pigs and poultry. The Romans did not invade but their vessels would have been seen off the coast ferrying provisions from Chester to the garrison on Hadrian's Wall.

THE EARLY CHRISTIANS

No one knows the exact date when Christianity was introduced but it happened some time in the fifth or early sixth centuries when missionaries, mainly from Ireland, were busy spreading their religious beliefs on the western side of the British Isles. St Patrick has been credited with converting the Manx but there is no written proof that he ever visited the Island. Whoever they were, the missionaries soon inspired the building of numerous little keeills (chapels) dedicated to St Patrick and other Celtic saints. More than 200 keeill sites have been discovered in all locations apart from marsh and high mountain land. A monastery was established at Maughold which became the main religious centre.

INVASION FROM THE NORTH

An era of quiet prosperity came to an end in AD798 when the first Viking longships began to plunder the coasts of Ireland and the Isle of Man. Masters of shipbuilding and seamanship, they set out in increasing numbers from the Scandinavian fjords or viks (hence Viking), those arriving in the Irish Sea coming mainly from Norway. The Celts resisted but were no match for the weapons and tactical skill of the invaders. Mann was an ideal base for Viking operations in the Irish Sea: sagas tell how the Norsemen would set off in early summer to raid the surrounding coasts and 'fare home to Mann' before the winter storms set in. These people were not barbarians: they had their own folklore, literature and music; they loved fine clothes, jewellery and ornaments; produced beautiful carvings in stone and wood and were skilled metalworkers. Above all, the Norse were exceptional organisers and their administrative legacy has endured in the Isle of Man for more than a thousand years.

Prior to 1079 and the reign of Godred Crovan ('King Orry'), the Island changed hands between a number of rulers. Viking chieftains conquered

DECORATIVE STONE SLAB SCULPTURE

More than 200 decorated slab-stones survive in the Isle of Man and some of the finest Celtic crosses can be seen at Maughold. Christianity brought with it advances in learning and in arts and crafts. Stone-slab sculpture of outstanding quality continued into the Norse period when the pagan newcomers were eventually converted to Christianity.

DANGERS OF KINSHIP

Magnus Haraldson, King of Mann, was one of the eight vassal kings who famously rowed King Edgar on the River Dee at Chester in 974. Magnus ranked second oar next to Kenneth of Scotland, but was killed four years later by the Irish king Brian Boroimhe. Many of the Manx kings paid a high price for their crowns and were either killed in battle or murdered.

and settled many coastal areas in the Irish Sea, supposedly in the name of the King of Norway but, in practice, they fought among themselves. In the reign of Godred I, strengthening links between Mann and the Hebrides led to the creation of the Kingdom of Mann and the Isles which was to play an important role in a power struggle between Norway, England and Scotland. Tynwald was established in 979 to administer this new, enlarged kingdom.

THE REIGN OF 'KING ORRY'

Godred Haraldson, an influential king from 978 to 989, may be the original 'King Orry' of legend but the man usually associated with the name is the warrior Godred Crovan, son of Harold the Black. Godred (the nickname 'Crovan' may refer to the white gauntlets he wore in battle) was used to conflict having fought alongside Harold Hardrada at Stamford Bridge against Harold of England in 1066, shortly before the fateful Battle of Hastings. Goree is the Manx form of Godred (hence 'King Orry') and Crovan is thought to have lived in the Isle of Man during his youth. According to tradition, he landed at the Lhen on a clear, starry night and, when asked where he came from, pointed to the Milky Way and said: 'Yonder is the road whence I came and along that star-spangled dome is the way that leads to my country'. Ever since, the Manx have called the Milky Way *Raad Mooar Ree Gorree* or 'Great Way of King Orry'.

Godred Crovan is also remembered for sparing the lives of the islanders who bravely opposed his invading army but were defeated at the Battle of Sky Hill, near Ramsey in 1079. Godred seized the throne by force but he reigned successfully for sixteen years and his dynasty endured until 1265. However, wars and internal quarrels progressively weakened the Manx kingdom – Mull and Islay were lost in the twelfth century. After a dispute with the King of Norway, Mann and the Scottish isles were formally ceded to Alexander III of Scotland in 1266. Magnus, the last Norse King of Mann, had died the previous year.

RETURN TO CHAOS

The Vikings made an indelible mark on the Isle of Man: they established a durable administrative system, intermarried with the Celts and eventually converted to Christianity. Unhappily, the period that followed their rule was to prove the most chaotic in Manx history with rapid changes of ownership reducing most of the native population to poverty and wretchedness. One vital institution prevailed – the Manx parliament. Before the loss of Mull and Islay, Tynwald consisted of 32 members, 16 from Mann and 16 from the Hebrides. When Scotland gained control, the 8 remaining Hebridean members were lost but the numbers were made up to 24 (as in the present House of Keys) by allowing 4 representatives from each of the Island's 6 divisions or sheadings.

Scottish rule was deeply unpopular and, in 1275, a vain attempt was made to restore the old Norse kingdom. For the next forty years, the Island was a prized pawn in the wars between England and Scotland because of its value as a naval base.

In 1313, after he had defeated Edward II, Robert the Bruce landed at Ramsey with a large army, marched to the nunnery at Douglas and then laid siege to Castle Rushen. After a month, the garrison was forced to surrender and the Scottish king took possession of the Isle of Man. It was all change again with the victory of Edward III over the Scots and, from that time on (apart from the republican Commonwealth years in the seventeenth century) the suzerainity of Mann has been invested in the English Crown. However, there was to be no stability until the people had endured yet another succession of petty rulers.

A HEAVY-HANDED CHURCH

With civil organisation in disarray, the church became increasingly powerful and oppressive. Religious houses, especially Rushen Abbey, acquired large tracts of land and enjoyed many valuable privileges. Courts

St German's Cathedral on St Patrick's Isle, Peel was founded in 1230 as the cathedral church of Mann and the Hebrides

DISTINCTIVE SURNAMES

Florrie Forde, the old music-hall star who frequently appeared in Douglas, used to sing about 'Kelly from the Isle of Man'. There have been plenty of Manx-born Kellys but, obviously, the name is not exclusive to the Island.

Characteristic Manx surnames have long been a delight (or headache) to philologists. They derive from a mixture of Celtic and Norse and the phonetic aspects of Manx Gaelic which in the past was primarily a spoken language. Many surnames begin with the letters C, K or Q: Corlett, Corkhill, Kerruish, Kermode, Quayle, Quine. This is the result of the prefix 'Mac' ('son of') being eroded leaving just the 'C' sound, as in Cubbon (MacGibbon), Quilliam (MacWilliam), Kissack (MacIsaac). However, the 'K' is silent in Kneen (MacNevyne) and Kneale (MacNele).

Opposite: Eleventh-century round tower, one of the oldest structures on St Patrick's Isle, probably built by monks to discourage invaders

Pages 36-7: Hugely popular with tourists in the last century, the Manx Electric Railway still links Douglas and Ramsey. This view shows the scenic line running parallel with the old coast road, north of Laxey

were held both by the abbot and the bishop who also appointed judges and maintained a prison in Peel. Tithes were levied on grain, livestock, dairy produce, fish, beer and much else. Caught between the indifference of the state and the demands of the church, the Manx people were sorely in need of stability. This arrived in 1405 in the shape of Sir John and Sir William Stanley, distinguished noblemen sent by Henry IV to secure the Island and hold it in his name. The following year Mann was granted to Sir John and his heirs on condition of paying homage and providing two falcons to all kings of England on their coronation.

STABILITY, THEN INSURRECTION

The Stanleys ruled until 1735, as Kings of Mann until 1504 and, thereafter, as Lords of Mann. They became Earls of Derby after helping to defeat Richard III at Bosworth in 1485. These lords lived for the most part on their estates in Lancashire but they did appoint responsible governors who tried to improve conditions for the people. Manx monasteries were suppressed soon after those in England but the Reformation was slower to progress owing to ignorance of the English language and the lack of books in Manx. Protestantism was accepted without bloodshed and has remained the dominant form of Christianity, strengthened by a powerful injection of Methodism in the eighteenth century. (John Wesley came twice and was impressed by the quality of the hymn singing.)

However, the Manx people felt that their time-honoured rights had been eroded and when the English Civil War broke out they turned against their Lord, James Stanley, the seventh Earl of Derby. Earl James (*Yn Stanlagh Mooar*, the great Stanley) managed to put down a rebellion in 1643 and to raise troops for the royal cause. He refused to surrender the Island even after Charles I had been executed and, in 1651, sailed to England with 300 troops in support of Charles II. He was captured at the decisive Battle of Worcester and eventually executed.

The Manx militia, led by able well-educated men, saw this as an opportunity to air their many grievances and to rebel against the Countess Charlotte who had been left in charge of Castle Rushen. They did not oppose the parliamentary commander Colonel Robert Duckinfield who arrived in Ramsey with 44 ships carrying 3 regiments of infantry and 2 troops of cavalry. Lacking support from the militia, the countess agreed to surrender the castle on condition that the defenders would be spared. One of the countess's principal officers, William Christian, assumed the leadership of the rebellion. Known as *Illiam Dhone* ('brown haired William'), he believed that resistance to the new republican Commonwealth would have cost many of his countrymen their lives and ancient liberties. Some called him a traitor but *Illiam Dhone* has gone down in Manx history as a brave patriot.

BISHOP THOMAS WILSON – FIERY BUT KIND

Bishop Wilson, born in Cheshire in 1663, lived to be 91 and was in office for 57 years. He was devoted to the Manx people and, in times of hardship, fed them out of his own resources. The bishop was a pioneer of universal education, compelling parents to send their children to school to learn English. On the down side, his desire to revive the old ecclesiastical courts and the cruel punishments meted out to 'sinners' brought him into conflict with the Manx state. At one point, Wilson and his two vicars-general were locked-up in Castle Rushen by the governor for attempting to incarcerate transgressors in the bishop's prison at Peel. He is buried at Kirk Michael.

RESTORATION AND RETRIBUTION

The restoration of Charles II in 1660 was bad news for William Christian, who was arrested when a general pardon granted by the king was said not to apply to the Isle of Man. William was executed by firing squad on Hango Hill, near Ronaldsway, after making a fine speech and declining a blindfold. A royal stay of execution arrived too late to save the Manx martyr but his name was eventually cleared and his estates restored to his family.

Ironically, the restoration of Charles Stuart was received with loud rejoicing in the towns of Peel, Ramsey, Castletown and Douglas. The Cromwellian regime had failed to deliver hoped-for reforms and there was a good deal of poverty in the Isle of Man. But as the seventeenth century wore on still the Manx crofters and fishermen found it increasingly difficult to pay tithes and to overcome a series of crop failures. Many emigrated and, when few new tenants came forward, Charles, ninth Earl of Derby (1672-1702), appointed Bishop Thomas Wilson to discuss the situation with the people and the House of Keys. The result was the Act of Settlement of 1704.

Known as the Manx Magna Carta, this legislation transformed the prospects of former tenants who, in effect, became landowners with rights of inheritance and sale. A fixed 'lord's rent' was still payable but impositions such as the supply of food and turf to the castles, were abandoned. The remaining lord's rights, subsequently acquired by the English Crown, were finally bought out by the Manx government in modern times.

'LAMENT FOR THE ISLE OF MAN'

When the tenth Earl of Derby died without issue, the lordship passed to the second Duke of Atholl, James Murray (1736-64), who encouraged the introduction of some much-needed reforms. An act, known as the 'Manx Bill of Rights', gave everyone the option of trial by jury and transferred to Tynwald the right to fix customs duties, once the prerogative of the Lord of Mann. Duties were much lower than in Great Britain which is why the Island became known as 'the very citadel of smuggling'.

Illicit and legal trade brought prosperity to those engaged in it and dubious 'foreign' entrepreneurs moved to Douglas to try their luck, some also attracted by the Island's lenient debt laws. Officialdom, including his lordship, turned a blind eye to smuggling on the grounds that Manx laws were not being broken. The British government fumed and fretted but was powerless to intervene until the third Duke of Atholl agreed to sell his sovereign rights to the Crown for a payment of £70,000, provided he could keep his considerable manorial privileges and receive an annuity of £2,000. (These privileges were purchased later from the fourth duke for the staggering sum of £416,114.)

As the following verse shows, the Manx people were less than happy with the deal:

> The babes unborn will rue the day
> That the Isle of Man was sold away;
> For there's ne'er an old wife that loves a dram
> But what will lament for the Isle of Man.

Draconian constitutional changes followed including a measure known as the 'Mischief Act' designed to stamp out 'the mischief of smuggling'. English customs officers were empowered to come into Manx ports and search suspect vessels; revenue offences could be tried in English courts and Manx merchants could only obtain dutiable goods from abroad via England. This was the last nail in the coffin of 'the running trade' – visiting speculators beat a hasty retreat and many 'respectable' Manx folk had to find other ways of making money.

A WELCOME INVASION

The nineteenth century transformed the fortunes of the Isle of Man, the economy being boosted by another invasion, this time a welcome one, by visitors and new residents. There had been regular weekly sailings to and from Whitehaven since 1767 but the inception of a Douglas-Liverpool service in 1819 was to prove a watershed. Between 1792 and 1821, the

THE LUCRATIVE MANX RUNNING TRADE

From the end of the seventeenth century until revestment in the English Crown in 1765 an immensely lucrative 'running trade' was conducted between the Isle of Man and the neighbouring countries. The Island's unique strategic and constitutional position meant that wines, spirits, tea, tobacco, spices and other commodities could be brought into Manx ports from abroad and, after the low local duty had been paid, smuggled to England, Ireland, Scotland and Wales. Speedy little ships were specially built to outrun the revenue cutters and land their contraband in isolated coastal inlets.

Opposite: Douglas harbour and Steam Packet ferry. The castellated building in the bay is the Tower of Refuge, a shelter for shipwrecked mariners

Ruined farm buildings are a reminder of the old crofting tradition which died out in the early part of the twentieth century

population grew from 27,000 to 40,000, boosted by an influx of ex-colonial officers retired on half pay and others attracted by the low cost of living and the beauty of the Island.

Summer visitors, mainly people from the English upper and middle classes, came in increasing numbers and tourism became a major source of revenue. Like their counterparts in Britain, Manx people continued to emigrate to America and the colonies but, by 1841, the population had risen to 48,000. Life was not easy for those who worked the land and fished the seas but, after the House of Keys became a popularly elected assembly in 1866 and Douglas succeeded Castletown as the capital, considerable progress was made in education, social and political reform. The Island's infrastructure was massively improved in Victorian times: fine harbours, good roads, elegant promenades and impressive houses and hotels were built; an island-wide network of steam trains and electric trams was established.

Crofting and fishing fluctuated and then declined towards the end of the nineteenth century. Investors did well out of the mining of lead, copper, iron and other minerals for many years but when profits fell the mines were closed. Visiting the Isle of Man became increasingly fashionable after Queen Victoria and Prince Albert came briefly in 1847 – the first of many visits by royalty. By 1860, annual visitor numbers had grown to 60,000 and in 1899 the figure climbed to 420,000, swollen by working-class families experiencing their first-ever holidays 'abroad'.

Many Manxmen were killed in action during the First World War, Manx ships and their crews saw distinguished active service and thousands of prisoners of war were interned on the Island. Between the wars, Tynwald increased its powers and there was a general improvement in the standard of living. In the 1920s and 1930s, visitor figures averaged above 500,000 annually, with peaks for the world-famous TT motorcycle races. The Second World War brought conscription for men (although many women volunteered) and so-called 'enemy aliens' were interned again, including exiled scientists, teachers, musicians and artists. The Isle of Man was extensively used for training purposes: the RAF had airfields at Jurby and Andreas and the Fleet Air Arm occupied Ronaldsway. Manx ships were in the thick of it once again – three were lost at Dunkirk and one in the North African operation in 1942. Manx servicemen and women served gallantly in theatres of war across the world.

BIG BUCKS AND HIGH TECH

The march towards greater self-determination and the restoration of the ancient rights of the Manx continued in the post-war period. The Manx government repurchased the lands sold to the English Crown by the fourth Duke of Atholl, took control of all ports and harbours, established an insular Post Office Authority, a Manx Customs & Excise Service and a 'freeport' at Ronaldsway. A separate Manx Telecom service was introduced and Manx Radio was the first on-shore commercial radio station in the British Isles. Increased prosperity has come from government initiatives, not least the encouragement of the finance sector through the provision of excellent facilities for international banking and investment. Most Manx people have benefited, and increasing numbers of new residents are happy to work or enjoy retirement in this independent, prosperous and largely unspoilt island.

4 DOUGLAS AND THE MANX TOWNS

DOUGLAS

Douglas (*Doolish*), population 24,000, is the capital of the Isle of Man, the power house of Manx prosperity and the main focus of government, business, shopping and entertainment. Almost half the population of the Island live in the Douglas-Onchan-Braddan conurbation: there is no shortage of employment for residents and no lack of things for visitors to see and do. A true Manxman would remind them that there is a lot more to the Isle of Man than the fleshpots of the capital but there is no denying that it is an attractive, flourishing town with an eventful history ('list to what the old bells say/the bells of Old Kirk Braddan').

By Manx standards, Douglas is an upstart: when Norse kings were making history in Castletown and Peel and invading armies were sailing into Ramsey Bay, it was an insignificant fishing hamlet. There were only fifty or so houses in 1511 and a meagre population of 810 in 1726. Then came the lucrative years of 'the running trade' when Douglas was the main base for the importation of spirits, spices and other goods from abroad which, after payment of the low Manx duties, were smuggled to the adjacent countries. After the trade was suppressed Douglas responded by expanding legitimate trade and the town continued to grow and prosper.

HOLIDAY DESTINATION

In 1830, the introduction of a regular steam-packet service between Douglas and Liverpool coincided with the new British concept of 'holidays', and led to the building of piers, promenades, hotels and guest houses in Douglas and other Manx resorts. The early tourists, upper- and middle-

Above: Old Kirk Braddan church, where outdoor services used to attract congregations of up to 20,000. A number of fine Norse crosses are on view
Left: Douglas Bay sparkles at nightfall – more Mediterranean than Manx

BESIDE THE SEASIDE

*In the music halls they sang
'Flanagan, Flanagan, take me to the
Isle of Man again' and between the
mid-nineteenth and mid-twentieth
centuries, millions of British tourists
experienced their first taste of 'going
abroad' when they landed at Douglas
(up to 45,000 in a single day). They
were seduced by one of the finest sea
approaches anywhere – the gently
curving bay between Douglas Head
and Onchan Head, sheltering 2 miles
(3km) of gleaming promenade lined
with elegant hotels and gardens. In
the background, the mysterious
mountains and green hinterland
were just asking to be explored.*

*The Government offices where the
House of Keys and Legislative Council
deal with the day-to-day business of
Tynwald*

class people accustomed to visiting seaside health resorts, were followed by
increasing numbers of working-class holidaymakers, mainly from the
north of England and Scotland, who packed the boarding houses, beaches
and dance halls.

After dark, the seafront continues to 'sparkle like a necklace' (as the old
brochures used to say) but there are fewer visitors to appreciate it. The
rapid growth of the financial sector has changed the appearance of the
town centre, where many shops and houses have been demolished to make
way for large office blocks bearing prestigious nameplates. Since the virtual
demise of the British bucket-and-spade holiday, tourism in the Isle of Man
has moved smartly upmarket with increased prosperity bringing an
improvement in the quality of hotels, shops, restaurants and bars. Much of
the old 'time enough' charm remains, however, and horse-drawn trams (the
oldest in the world) continue their leisurely way up and down Douglas
promenade.

'GIVEN OVER TO ENJOYMENT'

A much-travelled Victorian writer commented: 'There is not a town in
Europe so absolutely given over to enjoyment as Douglas in the month of
August. The very air breathes of it.' Modern Douglas has no desire to
emulate rowdy Ibiza but there is still plenty of enjoyment in the air. Pubs,
clubs, discos, restaurants, cinemas and a casino contribute to the capital's
nightlife. There are live shows at the Gaiety, a restored Victorian gem

designed by the celebrated theatre architect Frank Matcham, the 2,000 seater Villa Marina concert hall (open-air productions in the gardens), and 'Summerland' where there is also a cinema, a supervised children's play area, and roller skating.

A TASTE OF THE TOWN

Douglas is sufficiently compact to be explored on foot although buses come in handy when negotiating the steep hills leading to Upper Douglas. Most places of interest are easily reached from the 2 miles (3km) of promenade which in season is served by frequent horse-drawn trams. A good starting point is the tourist information office in the sea terminal at the southern end of the seafront, where over the years millions of steam-packet passengers have landed at the old Victoria Pier, 2,070ft (631m) in length, and the shorter King Edward VIII Pier (920ft/280m – and the only public structure named after the uncrowned king).

Before the first length of promenade gets into its stride, the Jubilee Clock Tower is the point where Victoria Street turns inland into the main business and shopping centre. On the right is narrow, busy Strand Street; on the left, at Prospect Hill, is Athol Street, lined with banks, insurance offices and advocates' chambers.

The government and legislative buildings are at the corner of Bucks Road and Finch Road with the House of Keys chamber on the ground floor, and the Tynwald Court and Legislative Council chamber above. Athol

IN THE SWIM

Sea bathing is available from quiet beaches which up to the 1950s were packed with holidaymakers. All-weather swimming is available at the 82ft (25m) competition pool, at the National Sports Centre on the outskirts of Douglas, which has a water lagoon area with flume features, a large indoor sports hall and a health and leisure suite. Outside is a stadium with an all-weather 6-lane running track and an 800m perimeter raceway for athletics and cycling.

Douglas promenade has retained much of its handsome Victorian façade, but many of the town's boarding houses have been demolished or converted to meet the demands of the finance sector

THE ISLE O
IN THE MIDDL

Street joins the main Peel Road near the steam-railway station which is at the top of the inner harbour where the River Douglas runs between the North and South Quays, the product of two rivers uniting a mile inland (Dhoo meaning 'dark' and Glass from *glais* meaning 'river'). From here it is a short step back to the bus station and sea terminal.

The sweep of seafront begins with the Loch Promenade from where there is a good view of the Tower of Refuge, erected in 1832 on the treacherous Conister Rocks in Douglas Bay. This shelter for shipwrecked sailors (boat parties can land at low water) was the brainchild of Sir William Hillary (1771-1847), who founded the Royal National Lifeboat Insitution and is on most people's list of heroes. Sir William's home – Fort Anne on Douglas Head, since demolished and replaced by an office block – was originally owned by an Irishman known as 'Buck' Whalley whose wife inherited a fortune on condition that she lived on Irish soil. Whalley solved the problem by importing tons of soil from Ireland and building Fort Anne on top of it – Douglas has never been a stranger to enterprise!

Loch Promenade (named after a former governor) was built in 1876-8 on land reclaimed from the sea and the attractive sunken gardens were part of a widening scheme in the 1930s. A few hundred yards along Loch Promenade is Regent Street, for the main post office (Manx stamps must be used on all letters) and rapid access to the shops in Strand Street and Castle Street. Strolling on, or riding on a horsetram, the next stretch is the Harris Promenade with the Gaiety Theatre and Villa Marina prominent. Church Street off the Harris Promenade is a quick way to reach St Thomas's Church – with fine frescoes by the gifted John Miller Nicholson – and the Manx Museum with the prizewinning 'Story of Mann' exhibition (see below). Broadway marks the start of the Central Promenade which continues as the Queen's Promenade to the Manx Electric Railway and horsetram terminii and Summerland leisure complex.

THE TREASURE HOUSE

The 'Story of Mann' presentation is a major attraction in the Island's Treasure House (*Thie Tashtee Vannin*), the Manx Museum and headquarters of Manx National Heritage. An insight into the Manx inheritance is gained through a series of imaginative, high-tech displays covering 10,000 years of history. More than £1.3 million has been spent in recent years redesigning and extending the museum's galleries, not least the impressive map room and an archaeology gallery voted Best in the British

THE NATIONAL ART GALLERY

In the same building as the Manx Museum is the National Art Gallery devoted to important examples of art in or about the Isle of Man. The Island's superb scenery and light has inspired numerous artists including John Miller Nicholson (1840-1913), arguably the best Manx-born painter, Archibald Knox (1864-1933), celebrated for his designs in silver and pewter for Liberty's, the prolific William Hoggatt (1879-1961) and contemporary artists such as Bryan Kneale RA whose three-legs sculpture can be seen outside Ronaldsway Airport.

Opposite: The Manx Museum where the award-winning Story of Mann presentation begins

Below: Part of a memorial window dedicated to the Manx poet T.E.Brown

Isles. There are frequent changes of specialist exhibitions throughout the year and a continuous programme of lectures and films.

The museum also houses the national archive of Manx printed works, manuscripts, photographs and films. Each year many thousands of residents and visitors make use of an advanced archival storage system to research history, landholdings, law, government, international trade, language, folklore and genealogy. Most of the Island's early written records have survived and in 1997 the Earl of Derby donated many invaluable documents covering the period when his family were the Lords of Mann.

DOUGLAS HEAD

The Department of Tourism has mapped out various town and heritage walks in and around Douglas. A trip to Douglas Head is almost *de rigueur* although hordes of visitors no longer crowd its slopes for open-air religious services and pierrot shows. Manx National Heritage has restored the Great Union Camera Obscura, built in the Victorian era and one of only four remaining in the British Isles. It offers spectacular views of the town and, according to the old publicity, opportunities to spy on unsuspecting lovers! From the 320ft (98m) vantage point of Douglas Head you can see the southern half of the Island and a range of hills from North Barrule, above Ramsey, to Bradda at Port Erin. Although no longer a through road, a marine drive runs south for 3 miles (5km) along the cliffs to Port Soderick, providing a taste of the Island's magnificent coastal scenery.

ONCHAN AND CAPTAIN BLIGH

Travelling north out of Douglas it is difficult to tell where the capital ends and the district of Onchan begins. This expanding dormitory village (population 8,500) has been looking after its own local affairs since 1895 and, in common with Laxey, Port Erin and other villages, is administered by a board of commissioners. Onchan derives its name from St Conachon or Conchenn ('dog head') and was a quiet little place until the post-war years. St Peter's Church, at the heart of the old village, was built in 1833 on the site of an

Left: Coastline at the end of the Marine Drive, Douglas
Right: Detail of decorative carving, Kirk Onchan

49

NORTH V SOUTH

In 1098 civil war broke out between the north and south divisions of the Isle of Man, culminating in a bloody conflict at Santwat Ford, near Peel. Rival chieftains Ottar and MacMarus both died in battle but the northerners prevailed thanks to the bravery of their women folk. As a reward Tynwald decreed: 'Of goods immovable the wives shall have half on the north side, whereas those on the south side shall receive only one third'.

Opposite: Mooragh Park, Ramsey

Below: Ramsey's Queen's Pier, where ferries used to dock, is being restored

earlier church where in 1781 Captain William Bligh, a Cornishman, married Elizabeth Betham, the daughter of a customs officer, stationed in Douglas. Eight years later Bligh was to share top billing with his Manx friend turned enemy, Fletcher Christian, in the dramatic mutiny on HMS *Bounty*. Lieutenant Edward Reeves, who fought with Nelson at Trafalgar and the poet T.J. Ouseley (*Mona's Isle*) are buried in Onchan churchyard.

ROYAL RAMSEY: 'SHINING BY THE SEA'

Ramsey (Norse *Ramsaa* = wild, garlic river), the second largest town in the Isle of Man and capital of the northern area, is described in song as 'Ramsey Town, O Ramsey Town, shining by the sea'. Viewed from the heights which surround it, the town often shines because, officially, this is the sunniest corner of the Island. Ramsey's magnificent bay, a 10-mile (16km) sweep from craggy Maughold Head to the low-lying Point of Ayre, has been favoured by royalty and invading armies ever since Godred Crovan ('King Orry') arrived in 1079 to conquer the Isle of Man.

Others seeking safe anchorage have included Somerled, Jarl of Argyll, who brought in 60 ships to overcome King Godred II; Rognavald, who in 1205 assembled a fleet of 100 war galleys for a raid on Ireland; Robert the Bruce, who landed a powerful force at Ramsey and marched on Castle Rushen; Colonel Duckenfield and his parliamentary troops during the English Civil War; King William III, on his way to the decisive Battle of the Boyne in Ireland; and Captain Elliot, who captured three enemy vessels after a running battle with the French in 1760.

A series of more benign visits began in 1847 with the unexpected arrival of Queen Victoria and Prince Albert. The queen stayed on board the royal yacht and received the Island's bishop while Albert went ashore. On a hill above the town, the Albert Tower commemorates the spot where the Prince Consort stood to admire the view. The town barber who took him there became a local celebrity but the governor was less fortunate: he arrived post-haste from distant Castletown only to see the royal yacht vanishing over the horizon! Since then the town has enjoyed official visits from successive British monarchs, hence the title 'Royal Ramsey'.

Douglas people have always been inclined to snort at such affectations because the north-south rivalry goes back to ancient disputes between the two halves of the Island. If the northerners won the only recorded battle between the sides, Douglas can point to the fact that it has long-since eclipsed Ramsey in terms of size and importance – even Onchan, the capital's satellite village has a larger population than Ramsey's 7,000.

In contrast to the conflict and excitement of the past, modern Ramsey is both a market town and a resort with an atmosphere all its own. A stroll up Parliament Street past the Regency-style courthouse is more old colonial than Manx in feeling. Ramsey is ideal for a quieter holiday (sailing,

ARTFUL ISLAND

Like other Celtic nations, the Isle of Man has a proud tradition promoting its arts and culture. International gatherings include Yn Chruinnaght Inter-Celtic Festival (July), Manannan Festival of Music & the Arts (June/July), Festival of Music & Dance (July/August), Manannan Opera Festival (September) and Jazz Festival (August). There is a continuous programme of music, arts, dance and drama events throughout the year.

There is no shortage of excellent walking country in the north of the Island

fishing, walking and golf) and is the perfect base for exploring the northern district. There are good shops, hotels, restaurants, pubs, sports facilities, heritage attractions and a full programme of events. Ramsey is the venue for the annual *Yn Chruinnaght* ('the gathering') Inter-Celtic Festival, held in July. This celebration of Manx music, dancing, literature and the arts is shared with performers from Ireland, Scotland, Wales, Cornwall and Brittany. There are ceilidhs, concerts, workshops and outdoor displays.

Ballure Church has a long history but there are not many ancient buildings in Ramsey – many of the old, narrow streets and cottages were destroyed by insensitive planners in the 1960s and 1970s. Ramsey is an active seaport where coasters load and unload bulk cargoes, and yachts and leisure craft gather in the tidal harbour. The shipyard has always had a reputation for quality engineering but the old salt works, which used to process brine piped from the Point of Ayre, has gone. Queen's Promenade leads from the harbour entrance, with its twin piers and lighthouse to the Queen's Pier, built to accommodate regular passenger services, now discontinued. Built in 1886, the pier was extended to a length of 2,300ft (701m) and provided with a 3ft (1m) gauge tramway.

From the West Quay, a swing bridge gives access to the popular Mooragh – 40 acres (16ha) of parkland filled with semi-exotic trees and

Grove House, near Ramsey – perfectly preserved since Victorian times.

shrubs plus a 12-acre (5ha) boating lake, created in the 1880s out of an unpromising expanse of sand and shingle. The park lies behind a promenade fronting a broad beach – one of many stimulating walks from Ramsey along the coastline or towards the town's dramatic backdrop, the North Barrule hills. Ramsey's river, the Sulby, rises near Snaefell and descends through a deep glen to the lowland plain and the sea. A tributary joins it from Glen Auldyn which begins close to the town. The coastline, running south to Laxey (for Snaefell mountain railway) and Douglas is 18 miles (29km) of scenic heaven best experienced on an MER tram. Faster travel to Douglas means following the famous TT course through Ramsey on to the mountain road.

Grove House, on the outskirts of Ramsey, is a magnet for those who love Victoriana. The villa and its contents have been lovingly preserved ever since Victorian times when it was the summer retreat of Duncan Gibb, a wealthy Liverpool shipping merchant and his family. His granddaughters, the Misses Janet and Alice Gibb, offered their home to Manx National Heritage so that their legacy could become a period museum. Most of the original furnishings and fittings have been retained in Grove House where costumes and family possessions covering three generations are on display. Early vehicles and agricultural equipment, including a restored horse-powered threshing mill, are housed in a series of outbuildings and the villa has fine gardens where ducks, hens and Manx cats roam.

SUNSET CITY OF THE WEST

I'm a native of Peel and I think for a meal,
That there's nothin' like priddhas and herrin',
I was rear'd on the quay, so I foller the say,
And it's middlin' good fishin' I'm getting.

In many ways, Peel is the most Manx of all towns. Built largely of local red sandstone its narrow winding streets are a reminder of the days when this was a leading fishing port employing thousands of men, the harbour packed with luggers, nickies and nobbies. Although few can remember the great fishing fleet sailing into a typical Peel sunset, fishing remains a useful part of a mixed economy which includes kipper-curing, chocolate manufacture and tourism. The quay, once lined with cheerful fisher girls, gutting and packing the 'herrin', is busy serving commercial and leisure craft. Peel is also the market town for the west side of the island.

Situated at the mouth of the River Neb, Peel (population 4,000) is known as a city because it was once the seat of the bishop. Its Manx name (*Purt-ny-Hinshey* = Port of the Island) refers to St Patrick's Isle at the mouth of the harbour where the remains of Peel Castle and St Germain's Cathedral create a dramatic silhouette when the sun goes down. St Patrick's Isle (reached by a short causeway) simply oozes history and is a major Manx National Heritage feature. When the focus of political power moved to Castletown in medieval times, Peel concentrated on fishing and agriculture. In the eighteenth century, smuggling put extra bread and a bit of silver on the town's table but it was the hard graft of fishermen and farmers that kept the 'sunset city' going. Peel's old streets are full of character and there are plenty of pubs, restaurants and specialist shops. Glen Maye, St John's and other places of interest are within easy reach.

MEET FLETCHER CHRISTIAN

The internationally acclaimed 'House of Manannan', an imposing structure built in Manx vernacular style on the harbourside at Peel, was opened in 1997 at a cost of £6 million and named Museum of the Year. Ingenious electronic-display techniques are used to explore the Celtic, Viking and maritime traditions of the island with Manannan, the mythical sea god and wizard, appearing in many guises in his role as official guide. There are full-size re-creations of a wooden roundhouse, occupied by a Celtic chieftain and his family, a stone Viking longhouse and an early Christian chapel. Other displays explain why Manx history is so inextricably bound up with

Peel – the view from the quiet end of the promenade

Sculpture outside the House of Manannan, Peel

FAMOUS MANX KIPPERS

To make kippers, herring are slit, gutted, soaked in vats of brine, then smoked on tenter hooks above smouldering wood chippings. The Manx claim to have a secret recipe for this process, hence the unique texture and flavour. (Photo IoM Tourism)

the sea through conquest, trade, travel, fishing and smuggling (once a lucrative source of income). There are reminders of famous Manx maritime connections, including Fletcher Christian who led the mutiny on HMS *Bounty* in 1789 and Capt William Bligh, cast adrift in an open boat by the mutineers. Christian came from a distinguished Manx family and although Bligh was not a Manxman, he was, as already mentioned, married in Douglas. Then there is the doughty Captain John Quilliam, one of Lord Nelson's favourite sailors who at the Battle of Trafalgar in 1805 steered HMS *Victory* from the gun room after the wheel had been shot away.

Tales of adventure and superstition feature Manx fishermen in home waters and sailors who travelled the world. A star exhibit is Odin's Raven, a two-thirds-size replica Viking longship built in Norway and sailed to Peel in 1979 to mark the millennium of Tynwald, the Island's parliamentary assembly. Those visiting the Isle of Man Steam Packet gallery are shown how they might command their own ship without any help from that old shapeshifter Manannan. Another section deals with the development and history of Peel; a delicious aroma of peerless Manx kippers, smoked over oak chippings, is part of the experience.

SECRETS OF ST PATRICK'S ISLE

Manannan also provides visitors with a personal electronic guide to St Patrick's Isle, now linked to Peel harbourside by a causeway. This place was a focus of Manx Christianity in the sixth century, a faith which survived the coming of the pagan Vikings at the end of the eighth century. The invaders recognised the Isle's defensive potential at the entrance to a good natural harbour and built defences which would later become Peel Castle, from which the town took its name.

Peel Castle was the seat of the early Norse rulers before Castle Rushen became the centre of administrative power. After the Island had reverted to the English Crown in 1765, the castle and its buildings fell into disrepair and even limited use ended in the nineteenth century. Peel Castle's curtain wall still surrounds the ruins of several buildings of secular and religious importance, including St Patrick's Church and a round tower from the eleventh century, and the thirteenth-century Cathedral of St German. According to the *Chronicles of the Kings of Mann*, St German's was founded in 1230 by Simon, Bishop of Sodor & Mann, as the cathedral church for the Sudreys (Mann and the Hebrides). After 1333, the cathedral was remodelled and the adjoining Vicars Chorale residential building was converted into apartments for occupation by successive Lords of Mann.

During the 1980s a six-year programme of archaeological excavation on St Patrick's Isle revealed many interesting artefacts now on display in the Manx Museum. The most striking find was the grave of a Viking woman of high birth complete with jewellery and other personal effects. These lovely ruins and their evocative setting have inspired many artists and writers, including Wordsworth who composed a poem to Peel Castle. Some eventful scenes in Sir Walter Scott's novel *Peveril of the Peak* take place on St Patrick's Isle and a tower is named after Fenella, a character in Scott's romance.

There are many superstitions associated with this place. A three-legged giant who lived there in the days of St Patrick was said to amuse himself by flinging large boulders of white quartz at the surrounding hills. Fragments can still be seen above Lherghydoo, 3 miles (5km) north of Peel. Fortunately, the giant jumped over Contrary Head and vanished into the sea. Another legend concerns the *Moddy Dhoo* (black dog) who haunted Peel Castle and terrified the garrison. One night a drunken soldier went alone into a dark passageway to challenge the apparition – dreadful screams were heard and the soldier was found wide-eyed and mad. He died three days later; the passageway was bricked up and the ghostly dog was never seen again.

St Patrick's Isle, with the ruins of Peel Castle and St German's cathedral

CASTLETOWN: THE OLD CAPITAL

CASTLE RUSHEN: AN ANCIENT SEAT OF POWER

Castletown (*Balley Chastal*), the centre of Manx political power until Douglas took over in the nineteenth century, is best known for Castle Rushen, home to the Kings and Lords of Mann. Built in the thirteenth and fourteenth centuries from hard local limestone – although the oldest parts date back to Norse times – Castle Rushen is one of the most complete and best-preserved castles in the British Isles. Many of the most intriguing and violent events in Manx history have taken place here. Before becoming a much-visited and admired showpiece, it served as a bulwark against invaders, an administrative centre, a law court, a mint and a prison (the frightful dungeons can still be seen). Today, the castle's dramatic story is told through figures in period costume and the atmospheric use of furnishings, wall hangings, medieval food, music and speech.

According to the *Chronicles of the Kings of Mann*, Magnus, the last Viking King of Mann, died here in 1265. The mouth of the Silverburn river was an obvious site for a fortification around which the ancient capital of Castletown grew up. Early defensive works would have consisted of an earth mound surrounded by stout wooden palisades. A stone, square keep was probably built during the reign of Godred II (1153-87) with the lower parts of the south and west towers being added in the time of Reginald I (1187-1286).

Castle Rushen survived capture by the Scottish king Robert the Bruce in 1313 and was eventually secured by English lords who embarked on a considerable programme of redevelopment. In the fourteenth century, existing towers were heightened and an east tower, gatehouse and curtain wall added. Successive rulers continued to reinforce the castle, and Welsh

Ancient Castle Rushen is the unlikely setting for the Island's annual International Jazz Festival (IoM Tourism)

craftsmen may have helped because some sandstone doorways and windows closely resemble those found in other castles in North Wales. In 1377 the French attacked but the castle was well able to withstand a siege.

As Peel Castle declined Castle Rushen came to represent the power of the Kings and Lords of Mann. After the Earls of Derby became overlords in 1405, the castle was the main centre of administration and the seventh earl lived in Derby House, an existing building extended in 1644. The Manx rebelled against the earl during the English Civil War, and in 1651 the royalist Countess of Derby was forced to surrender Castle Rushen to the parliamentary forces. This episode led to the controversial trial and execution of the Manx patriot William Christian (*Illiam Dhone*) following the restoration of Charles II.

The centre of Castletown is little changed since the eighteenth century

THE TOWN

Castletown (population 3,000) stands at the mouth of the Silverburn river which empties into a snug corner of Castletown Bay. The delightful tidal harbour is best suited to small vessels which explains why Derbyhaven, on the other side of the Langness peninsula, was often the preferred port in the past. Most of the town's historic buildings are grouped around the harbour including the Old Grammar School, the oldest roofed building in the Island. This small, whitewashed structure was built in the thirteenth

century as St Mary's Chapel, but was a school from 1570 to 1930 and the forerunner of King William's College.

When Castletown was the home of both the governor and the Manx parliament, members met in the Old House of Keys, which has been restored by Manx National Heritage so that visitors may learn about the Island's unique political history. A footbridge across the harbour leads to the Nautical Museum and *Peggy*, an eighteenth-century armed yacht, discovered walled-up in a boat cellar in 1935. Built in 1791, she had lain undisturbed for a hundred years after the death of her owner, the eccentric Captain George Quayle.

These three buildings are marked on the Castletown Heritage Trail which also takes in the 'Candlestick' (a memorial to Governor Cornelius Smelt which lacks his statue) erected on the site of the old market cross where a woman and her son were burned as witches in 1617. Close by is the Old Town Hall, a former barracks; the elegant eighteenth-century George Hotel; a house where Captain Quilliam of Trafalgar fame lived; the Old Steam Packet building and the unusual police station designed by the world-famous architect Mackay Hugh Baillie Scott (1864-1945).

Unspoiled and well preserved is the only way to describe Castletown. The days when Castle Rushen was under siege and the Lords of Mann issued edicts to the people are long gone and the town has moved with the times: there are two pedestrianised shopping streets to complement the open-air market, an indoor swimming pool and a choice of pubs and restaurants. Scarlett Visitors' Centre and Nature Trail is not far away while Langness, Derbyhaven and St Michael's Isle are just the other end of Castletown Bay.

SAND AND SAILING

I'm the pride of Port le Murra, I can reap or plough or furra',
I can find the gentle lugworm in the sand.
I am up to all that's tricky in the sailing of a Nicky,
An' I'm toul' there's not my aiquel in the land.

Port Erin and Port St Mary are quiet holiday resorts which have attracted many new residents in recent years – Port Erin has a population of approximately 3,500 and Port St Mary 2,000. Between them these pretty villages epitomise the best of relaxing sand and sailing holidays. Port Erin (*Purt Chiarn*) is tucked away in a deep indentation on the south-west coast and is the nearest port to Ireland. The unusually square bay is an inviting

Modern vessels anchor close to the medieval castle at Castletown

safe haven flanked by lofty headlands: Bradda to the north, Castle Rocks to the south.

A sweep of sandy beach backed by a long promenade offers some of the best and safest bathing in the Island. In every direction the outdoors beckons: scuba diving, sailing, pony trekking, coastal walks. Port Erin is the home of the important Marine Research Laboratory (which can be visited) and of the Erin Arts Centre, venue for the Manannan international festival of music and the arts. This is also the southern terminus of the vintage steam-railway service from Douglas via Castletown.

Port St Mary (*Purt-le-Moirrey*) is little more than a mile from the centre of Port Erin but it has managed to retain the character of an old fishing village. There is a working harbour, frequented by visiting yachts and pleasure craft, a good breakwater and a safe sandy beach at Chapel Bay. Few fishing vessels take advantage of the deep-water berths these days but queenies, a local shellfish delicacy, are processed in the village. Pubs and restaurants are noted for their home cooking.

Port St Mary is the best centre for boating excusions to the Sugarloaf rock, Spanish Head and the Calf of Man. It is also ideally placed for walks to the Mull hills, Cregneash Folk Village and along the coastline. The views over land and sea have inspired generations of artists, photographers and the senders of heartfelt 'wish you were here' postcards.

Cregneash (Gaelic for 'rock of ages') is a village which may have been settled for thousands of years. It looks much as it did in the nineteenth century when traditional crofting skills were practised and Manx was the everyday language. Part of the village is a folk museum managed by Manx National Heritage. The value of preserving this delightful unspoiled hamlet was recognised as far back as 1938 when the Manx Museum was presented with Harry Kelly's cottage and opened it to the public. Harry is remembered as the old crofter who made the first sound recordings of Manx speech for a Norwegian Professor of Celtic – Carl Marstrander.

Other buildings in Cregneash and large areas of the surrounding countryside have been preserved to provide an authentic picture of life in a typical Manx upland crofting community. Visitors can see fields being worked with horse-drawn implements, roof thatching, wool dyeing, spinning, weaving, wood turning and blacksmithing. They may also sample Manx food freshly prepared in the old white-washed cottages.

MANX MENU

Manx speciality food is served in pubs, cafes and restaurants all over the Island. Locally caught seafood delicacies include Queen scallops, lobster, crab and a variety of really fresh fish (even in chip shops). The famous oak-cured kippers are eaten any time of day, plain or with butter or marmalade! Manx lamb is succulent and has featured on 'Master Chef'. Other specialities are bonnag (large scones, plain or with fruit), blaeberry pie, 'real' Manx ice-cream, full flavoured cheeses, delicious preserves and a range of traditionally brewed local beers. An International Food & Drink Festival is held annually.

Opposite: Port St Mary

Below: Crofter's cottage, Cregneash – restored, but the real thing

'LAXEY WHEEL KEEPS TURNING, TURNING, TURNING'

Below: 'Lady Isabella'

Opposite above: Laxey Station on the Manx Electric Railway line between Douglas and Ramsey, is the terminus for the Snaefell Mountain Railway (IoM Tourism)

Opposite Below: Glorious gardens in Laxey Glen

Laxey (Norse *Laxa* = salmon river), an old mining village on the coast between Douglas and Ramsey, has been transformed in recent years. Until the eighteenth century it was no more than a cluster of fishermen's cottages near the harbour. After valuable mineral deposits were found, a new village was built higher up on the slopes of Laxey Glen and more than 600 men were employed when mining was at its peak. In 1857 Laxey was the main source of zinc blende in the British Isles, in addition to producing lead ore rich in silver. Towards the end of the nineteenth century the industry began to decline and the mines finally closed in 1929.

Laxey's industrial scars have healed and the village, in its lush green setting, is now a pleasant place to live. Thousands come here to see 'Lady Isabella', the largest working waterwheel in the world. The Great Laxey

Wheel is a Manx symbol almost on a par with the Three Legs of Man. Built in 1854 and named after the then-governor's wife, it was designed by the engineer Robert Casement to pump water from the Glen Mooar section of the Laxey Mines industrial complex. 'Lady Isabella' has a circumference of 277ft (84m), a diameter of 77ft (23m) and a viewing platform on top reached by 95 steps. However, the wheel is no longer required to pump 250 gallons (1,137 litres) of water per minute or to dispose of it through channels linked to washing floors lower down the valley.

In 1965 the Laxey Wheel was bought by the Manx Government and restored to its former glory. The neighbouring area of Glen Mooar was also purchased and, after extensive surveys and clearance work, the Laxey Mines Trail was opened, as part of the national heritage programme. It provides an insight into the hardship and danger endured by the men who dug deep for lead, copper, zinc and silver. There was little gold in 'them thar' Manx hills but fortunes were made, at least by the investors. People can also visit the woollen mills, the lovely glen and gardens and travel to the top of Snaefell on the mountain railway which starts from leafy Laxey station.

5 LEGACY OF THE PAST

ANYONE INTERESTED in the physical evidence of the past will want to visit at least some of the historic sites found throughout the Isle of Man. They are among the most important in Europe and include the remains of prehistoric settlements, burial chambers, early churches, forts and the largest known concentration of Celtic and Norse cross-slabs.

The most substantial and influential medieval religious site in the Island is Rushen Abbey, acquired by the Manx government in 1998 and, since Easter 2000, the focus of another imaginative MNH presentation. Visitors can learn about life in a flourishing Cistercian community, walk through surviving parts of the abbey and follow the progress of ongoing archaeological research on site, via a live video link.

Several Norse kings were buried in Rushen Abbey, including Magnus, the last King of Mann & the Isles. By the end of the Norse period, the abbey owned ninety-nine quarterland farms, with many mills and cottages. It survived a sacking by Irish raiders in 1316 when it was 'despoiled of all its furniture, its oxen and sheep, leaving nothing at all'. The powers of the abbot were curbed by the Stanley family who became Lords of Mann in 1405 and, after the dissolution of religious houses in the sixteenth century, much of the abbey stone was taken for use in other buildings. Fortunately, the *Chronicles of the Kings of Mann & the Isles* survives from the days when this was the centre of culture in the Isle of Man.

Rushen Abbey, now a Manx Heritage attraction, was a major influence before the Reformation

MANX BEST SELLER

An impressive tomb in Maughold churchyard marks the last resting place of the writer Sir Thomas Henry Hall Caine (1853–1931) whose stories sold in their millions and were translated into twenty languages. Many of his melodramatic novels and plays became popular silent films. Hall Caine loved his native island but was mistrusted by ordinary Manx folk who said 'he made his living telling lies!'

READING THE RUNES

Cast copies of 204 decorated stones are kept in the Manx Museum and the majority of the originals can be seen in the churches and churchyards of the parishes where they were found. Preserved in the museum is the Calf of Man Crucifixion, a fine example of Celtic Christian art. This fragment, found in the ruins of a keeill (early chapel) on the Calf islet in 1773, is thought to have been part of a shrine or an altar front. Crosses have served as grave markers and memorial stones in the Island since the fifth century AD. Celtic designs vary from a simple cross motif to beautiful, complex interlacing with inscriptions in Celtic ogham lettering or, occasionally, Latin. Some of the finest are on view at Kirk Maughold and there are others at Old Kirk Braddan and Onchan parish church. A tenth-century wheel-headed cross-slab, probably in its original position at Old Kirk Lonan, near Laxey, is particularly impressive.

After the invading Vikings had converted to Christianity, there was a merging of cultures with figures from pagan mythology also appearing on memorial stones. The most influential Norse sculptor was Gaut, who used the distinctive ring-chain patterning and worked on the Island during the tenth century. There are runes from this period which suggest intermarriage between Celtic and Norse families.

Kirk Maughold Cross House

PAGAN CHIEFTAINS AND CELTIC MONKS

One of the best-preserved Neolithic chambered tombs is *Cashtal yn Ard*, situated on raised land overlooking the old parish of Maughold (pronounced 'mackel') which is easily reached from the coast road a few miles south of Ramsey. Neolithic chieftains were laid to rest here around 3000BC. Access to a burial chamber with five compartments is gained through a portal of two standing stones leading from a semi-circular forecourt. Although the monument is no longer covered by a 130ft (40m) oblong cairn, enough giant stones remain to create a dramatic effect. Unburnt human bones, pottery and flints have been found on the site.

Mann's most important Celtic monastery was established at Maughold in early Christian times. It covered an area now defined by the graveyard of Kirk Maughold church where the foundations of three keeills and the sites of two others have been discovered. There were probably several earlier buildings on the site of the present church which has part of an eleventh-century Irish Romanesque arch reset in the west doorway and small thirteenth-century windows in the south wall.

A remarkable collection of cross-slabs from the seventh to eleventh centuries, all found in the vicinity, are preserved in a churchyard cross-shelter. Among the Celtic specimens is the Crux or Cross of Guriat, whose

Pages 70-1: Cashtal yn Ard, Maughold – one of the largest Neolithic burial sites of its kind in the British Isles

Below: St Maughold's Well, where the saint baptised his followers. Sick people believed in its curative powers

Above: St Maughold's Well and many other places of interest can be reached from the coastal footpath

Opposite: Chapel Hill boat burial, Balladole

Below: Thorleif Hnakki's cross stands out among other cross-slabs at Braddan

son Myrfyn established a dynasty of kings in North Wales. It dates from the eighth century and measures 7ft (2m) and almost 3ft (1m) in width. Raised hemispherical bosses protrude from the face of this massive stone to symbolise a cross-head. Another Celtic slab, carved in low relief with a ring-headed cross and a saint seated on each side of the cross-shaft, has similarities to Pictish carvings in Scotland.

VIKING HEROES

Scenes from heroic Norse tales appear on later monuments: Loki throwing a stone to kill Otter, the great fisher (Maughold); Sigurd slaying a dragon with his sword (Jurby); Odin devoured by the Fenris wolf (Andreas); the maid Gerth and the god Frey who wooed her (Michael). Standing before these legendary scenes you can almost hear the strains of Wagnerian music. Other Viking crosses are more Christian than pagan: Thorlief Hnakki's cross (Old Braddan church), a tapering pillar with a pierced-ring cross-head, combines interlaced dragon motifs with a runic inscription: *Ihsus* ie 'Jesus'.

Maughold is a delightful little country hideaway. There is a holy well a half-mile from the village and the views from Maughold Head, both inland and seawards, are exceptional. Legend has it that St Maughold had been a wicked Irish robber who did penance by launching his coracle onto a stormy sea. Instead of drowning, as expected, he was washed ashore at Maughold where he founded a monastery to celebrate his deliverance. In the unlikely event of there being any truth in this tall tale, the rogue turned saint certainly picked a beautiful spot.

VIKING SHIP BURIALS

Evidence of occupation over thousands of years has been found at Chapel Hill, Balladoole, near Castletown. Excavations have revealed prehistoric flints, Bronze Age burials and earthworks from the Iron Age, early Christian stone lintel graves and the foundations of a keeill dedicated to St Michael, dating from the tenth or eleventh century. Most spectacular of all the finds was a pagan boat burial of the late ninth century or early tenth century. In the boat lay the richly adorned body of a Viking warrior or well-to-do farmer, accompanied by the remains of a woman. His horse and livestock had been sacrificed so perhaps the lady was also expected to accompany her lord and master to Valhalla!

A similar fate may have overtaken a young woman whose skeleton was found in a Viking burial mound at Ballateare, Jurby, excavated by the German archaeologist Gerhard Bersu in 1946: the back of her skull had been removed by a hard blow administered by a sharp weapon. She was found with typical grave goods and a layer of cremated animal bones. The

'KING ORRY'S GRAVE'

The largest megalithic monument in Mann is the 170ft (52m) chambered cairn near Laxey, known as 'King Orry's Grave', although the site predates the legendary Viking king by more than 4,000 years and is the burial place of Neolithic chieftains. The site was cut in two by a roadway long ago and most of the covering cairn was removed. A single-chambered tomb, from roughly the same period, can be seen in a field on Ballachrink farm at Ballakelly, Santon.

Above: King Orry was probably buried on the island of Islay

Opposite: Part of the megalithic burial site on Meayll Hill, near Port Erin. Bradda Head is in the distance

value of this excavation was enhanced when a cemetery site of the Neolithic 'Ronaldsway' culture was found beneath and around the Viking mound. Another Viking ship burial was found at Knock y Doonee, Andreas, in 1927 and three other distinctive burial mounds of the Norse period have been discovered in nearby Jurby.

HOUSING THE DEAD

Meayll Hill, near Cregneash Folk Village, was occupied from Neolithic to medieval times. There is a megalithic tomb of unique design with six pairs of burial chambers arranged in a 60ft (18m) circle, with a passage leading inwards to the junction of each pair. Pottery shards, a jet bead and flints, including leaf-shaped arrow heads, have been found but this is believed to be a much-robbed cairn. It is worth climbing the hill just for the panoramic views across the south of the island.

An early Bronze Age burial site known as the 'Giant's Grave', at St John's, German, is exposed by a road cutting through the original mound. The Arragon *Mooar* stone circles in Santon are the remains of two prehistoric burial mounds in adjacent fields where some of the larger boulders, in a roughly circular setting, are of white quartz. The round Corvalley Cairn of early Bronze Age type, just south of Glen Cam in German, has a narrow opening which leads into a cist formed of massive blocks of white quartz. More difficult of access is the cairn marking a large Neolithic or early Bronze Age burial mound on the summit of Cronk ny Iree Laa in Rushen, 1,499ft (457m) above sea level.

Also worth noting are the Giant's Quoiting Stone at Ballacreggan, Port St Mary, an imposing single standing stone, 10ft (3m) high, probably of late Neolithic date, and the Spiral Stone at Ballaragh, Lonan, a granite boulder decorated with spiral patterns.

THE CELTS AND NORSE AT HOME

A model reconstruction of two Celtic Iron Age homesteads at Ballakeigan, Arbory, can be seen in the Manx Museum in Douglas. These houses were occupied from the third century BC to the first century AD and were large, circular timber-framed buildings about 90ft (27m) in diameter. Not far from Douglas, on the road to Foxdale, is the Braaid where the stone foundations of an Iron Age roundhouse and the succeeding Norse homestead and byre have been found. There are similar sites at Ballanorris, Arbory; Cashtal Lajer, Ballaugh; and the so-called Manannan's Chair, near the Staarvey Road, an ancient ridgeway leading from Tynwald Hill to Kirk Michael.

FORTIFICATIONS

As you would expect in an Island which was once surrounded by enemies on all sides, there is no shortage of defensive fortifications. They range from the Iron Age promontory fort at Cronk ny Merriu on Santon Head (re-occupied by the Vikings) to the Stanleys' circular stone Derby Fort on St Michael's Isle, near Derbyhaven. Built in 1540, the fort was refurbished in 1645 by James, seventh Earl of Derby. Close by is the ruined Chapel of St Michael's, typical of the twelfth century and probably built on the site of an earlier keeill.

There are much older clifftop fortifications at nearby Cass ny Hawin, consisting of a ditch and rampart from the Celtic Iron Age and the outline of a large, rectangular Norse-style house. There are ancient promontory forts, some defending their landward sides, at Burroo Ned, Rushen; Langness peninsula; Close ny Chollagh, Scarlett, Malew; and Ballanicholas, Marown. Cleigh yn Arragh, in Lezayre, is a massive bank and ditch built to defend the western portion of the Lhergy Rhenny ridge from attack from the hills.

Enthusiasts prepared for a stiff climb and a trudge over rough moorland can reach the largest and highest hill fort on the island – the summit of South Barrule at 1,585ft (483m). Traditionally known as 'Manannan's Castle', this is a typical Celtic tribal hill fort of circa 500BC, with numerous hut circles enclosed by a huge dry-stone rampart. Also from the Celtic period, but more accessible, is Cronk Sumark in Lezayre, a fortified rocky hill with an outer rampart of stone blocks partly fused by intense heat. A smaller enclosure or 'citadel' may mark a later Norse fortress. A 'citadel' is also a feature of the Castleward hill fort, an isolated rocky hillock in the valley of the River Glass in Braddan, dating back to the first century BC. Again, the ramparts are vitrified in places.

THE HERMIT'S CELL

The most isolated of all Manx keeills is Lag ny Keeilley ('hollow of the chapel'), which lies at the southern end of the MNH property of Eary Cushlin in Patrick. Those prepared to follow an old pack-horse track will reach the ruins of a chapel, a hermit's cell, a burial ground and the Chibbyr y Vashtee ('well of the baptism'), one of many holy wells with a tradition of healing powers.

EARLY CHRISTIAN CHAPELS

The earliest keeills were built of wattle and daub but those that have survived, probably from the eighth to twelfth centuries, have earth walls faced with stone. They are very small, rectangular buildings averaging about 16ft (5m) by 10ft (3m). Sometimes, the foundations of an altar remain at the east end. Lonan Old Church, near Laxey, a tiny former parish church still used for special occasions, retains traces of twelfth-century work built on the foundations of a much earlier keeill.

St Trinian's Chapel, a roofless, ruined church, near Crosby on the main Douglas-Peel road is the fourteenth-century enlargement of a chapel built in 1200 on the site of another keeill. The original name was St Ninian's and in 1780 material was taken from the chapel to build Marown church on the

south side of Crosby. Manx folklore offers a much more sinister explanation for the roofless chapel: the presence of an evil spirit known as a Buggane, which blew the roof off each time workmen attempted to erect it. A suggested solution was for the village tailor to make a pair of breeches before the Buggane could strike again but the poor fellow ran out of thread and the Buggane blew extra hard and neither the tailor nor the roof were ever seen again.

Some of the best-preserved keeills are in the Marown area: Keeill Vreeshey (St Bridget's Chapel), on Eyreton farm, near Crosby; Cabbal Druiaght (Druids' Chapel) on Glenlough farm, between Union Mills and Glen Vine; Keeill Pherick (St Patrick's Chapel) at Ballafreer, near Union Mills and the keeill at Ballaquinney, Glen Vine. There is another St Patrick's Chapel with ruins of a hermit's cell and a burial ground at Spooyt Vane, Glen Mooar, Michael. Moving on to a sacred place of later date, the Friary Chapel in Arbory is little changed from the time of its foundations by Irish Franciscans in 1367. After the Reformation, the chapel was preserved within a group of farm buildings 300 yards (274m) south of Arbory church (visitors should obtain permission before gaining access).

Top: Mysterious St Trinian's Chapel, Crosby

Above: Keeill Vael, Balladoole may date from the tenth century

6 EXPLORING 'THE FAIR ISLE'

And the fair isle shines with beauty
As in youth it dawned on me –
My own dear Ellan Vannin
With its green hills by the sea.

(*Ellan Vannin* – Manx song)

THE ISLE OF MAN IS UNRIVALLED in the British Isles for a variety of fine scenery in a comparatively small area which can be explored on foot, bicycle, car, public transport or a combination of travel modes. Although a motorist, sticking to the main coastal routes, could drive round the Island in half a day there are many hundreds of miles of roads and lanes. More than 40 per cent of the Island is uninhabited and it would take a lifetime to explore the entire landscape.

WALKS ON THE WILD SIDE

Away from the towns, the Manx countryside is little altered since the 1890s when T.E. Brown wrote: 'My walk yesterday, a good twelve miles across mountains, finished in a labyrinth of lovely glens: they smelt of heaven, so indeed did the mountains.'

Walking means the right to roam, almost untramelled, in terrain which embraces long stretches of sand and shingle, wetlands teeming with wild life, imposing hills, hawk-haunted moors, wooded glens and a stunning coastline. To make the most of numerous options (from signposted long-distance paths to short rambles) walkers need at least one or more maps, preferably those of the Ordnance Survey, the IoM Public Rights of Way, or the Official Tourist Map of the IoM.

For those who do not want to plan their own itineries, there are guided walking holidays, inclusive of accommodation, meals and transport to and from all start and finish points. A typical week might include five guided walks each of between 7 miles (11km) and 10 miles (16km), allowing plenty of time to visit places of interest along the way.

Above: Sulby Glen extends for 10km (6 miles)

Opposite: Maughold Lighthouse – one of five around the Manx coast

RAAD NY FOILLAN (ROAD OF THE GULL)

Those looking for a challenge can tackle the guided coastal trek of 96 miles (155km) in a week which earns those who complete it a certificate of achievement. These energetic folk follow the Raad ny Foillan (Road of the Gull), 'the long walk around the Island', created in the Manx Heritage Year of 1986. A less intense way of tackling this fine coastal footpath is to walk it in stages. The way is clearly marked with a gull on a blue sign and, wherever possible, it follows the entire coastline over terrain which varies from lonely shingle beaches to massive windblown cliffs alive with seabirds.

The Heritage Trail follows a disused railway line between Douglas and Peel

THE MILLENNIUM WAY

Experienced hikers can walk the Millennium Way (established in 1979 to mark the thousand years of Tynwald) from Castletown over the mountains to Ramsey in a day. Less intrepid walkers may cover it in three convenient legs, using public transport to leave or join the path at different places. The mountain section can be wild and woolly and, on breezy days, it is as well to check the direction of the wind before deciding on a starting point.

The Millennium Way is clearly signposted throughout its 28 miles (45km) along the ancient 'Regia Via', the Royal Way to Ramsey. It starts officially from Castle Rushen and finishes at Sky Hill (scene of a historic battle) a mile from Ramsey town square. The route takes in some pretty scenery through Ballasalla, Silverdale Glen, Crosby and the magnificent Baldwin valley before traversing the aptly named 'Plains of Heaven' into the rugged uplands (heather-purple and gorse-yellow in autumn), to skirt Snaefell and then descend between Sulby Glen and Glen Auldyn. Before there were roads suitable for wheeled transport, these old upland tracks were worn smooth by convoys of pack-ponies and sturdy little Manx horses drawing heavily laden sleds.

BAYR NY SKEDDAN (THE HERRING ROAD)

Bayr ny Skeddan is 14 miles (23km) in length, clearly marked with a blue sign incorporating a herring, and is the way Manx fishermen used to travel between Castletown and Peel. If it was dark they would sing to discourage evil spirits. Their road follows the Millennium Way as far as Silverdale Glen, then turns north over moorland close by South Barrule – 1,585ft (483m), the highest point in the south of the Island – and descends to Glen Maye to join the Raad ny Foillan for the final 3 miles (5km) into Peel. South Barrule occupies an important place in Manx history and folklore: its name in old Norse is *Vardar-fjall* ('Watch Fell') but there was a hill fort on its summit before the Iron Age. Old wives' tales tell of mysterious goings-on in a castle, the last occupant being a wicked magician who made the building disappear. The ascent is easily made from the Herring Road at the Round Table, the summit of the pass between Cronk-ny-Irey-Lhaa and South Barrule.

THE HERITAGE TRAIL

Easier to walk is the 10.5-mile (17km) Heritage Trail which follows a disused railway line from Quarterbridge, Douglas, through pleasing countryside to Peel, running close to the A1 which makes for easy access to Glenlough Keeill and spooky St Trinian's Chapel. St John's is at the crossroads of several main routes linking the main towns and has been the site of public assemblies for more than a thousand years. In early July, the ancient Court of Tynwald assembles on Tynwald Hill (a modest tiered mound) to enable new laws to be promulgated in both English and Manx. This is a colourful festival day celebrating the independence and traditions of the Manx nation.

A WEALTH OF WALKS

Another old-railway path from Peel to Ramsey follows the Raad ny Foillan for 16 miles (26 km) before turning east just beyond Kirk Michael. The way goes on through Ballaugh, Curragh Wildlife Park, Sulby (with access to Sulby Glen) and on to Ramsey, with the northern hills on one side and the lowland plain on the other.

The main long-distance footpaths are useful for accessing other rural walks and can be enjoyed piecemeal at a leisurely pace. Here are some examples: Port Erin to Castletown, 12 miles (19km) of exceptional coastal walking with diversions to Cregneash Folk Village, Port St Mary and Scarlett Visitor Centre; Douglas to Port Soderick, a 5-mile (8km) stroll through a glen to the beach and along a marine drive with some unusual rock formations; Peel to Port Erin, on the Road of the Gull with diversions to Glen Maye, Niarbyl, Lag ny Keilly hermitage, Cronk ny Irey Lhaa (Hill of

Approaching Port Soderick, south of Douglas

the New Day) and finishing with a steep climb to the top of Bradda Head.

Manx towns and villages are starting points for many recognised walks. From Ramsey to the Ayres is an 8-mile (13km) circular route along lanes, sand dunes and beaches, taking in the Ayres Visitor Centre and Nature Trail. Short walks around Ramsey include the ascent through pretty woodland to the Albert Tower – 500ft (152m) above the town with views of the English and Scottish coasts – and the Claughbane footpath leading to Glen Auldyn which extends for 4 miles (6km) into the heart of the mountains.

Laxey to the top of Snaefell and beyond can be tackled in various ways: on foot through Glen Roy (with the glorious Ballalheannagh gardens) or by mountain railway to the summit and then descending through Tholt-y-Will and Sulby Glen or via Beinn-y-Phott and Barregarrow (where John Wesley preached) to Kirk Michael on the Peel-Ramsey bus route.

Steep paths lead from Peel's West Quay to Corrin's Tower, a landmark perched 500ft (152m) up the hillside. After an initial climb the path levels off along the clifftops continuing along the edge of Contrary Head overlooking the sea. The tower, known locally as Corrin's Folly, is a solid, square building, 50ft (15m) high and built in 1806 with four floors and an internal stone stairway. To demonstrate his non-conformist belief that there is no shame in being interred in unconsecrated ground, Corrin arranged for himself, his wife and children to be buried near the tower. From the top of his 'folly', the view south takes in the coastline to Bradda Head and the Calf of Man. To the north, beyond Peel, are the lower cliffs and the plains of Ayre with a glimpse of the Mull of Galloway on a clear day.

From Castletown, the Silverdale trails follow the Silverburn river through Great Meadow to Ballasalla (steam train and bus stops) with Rushen Abbey and the family attractions of Silverdale Glen nearby. Castletown Bay is bounded on the east by the peaceful Langness peninsula noted for its wildlife, history and golf. A walk of half a mile round the bay leads to Hango Hill, a small mound where the Manx patriot William Christian (*Illiam Dhone*) was executed in 1663. Nearby is King William's College, a distinguished public school opened in 1833 whose grounds adjoin Ronaldsway airport. Derbyhaven bay, an excellent natural harbour at the lower end of the peninsula, was a favourite landing-place in ancient times and is still popular with sailors and fishermen. Several bloody battles were fought on its shores between rival Viking chiefs but the one most lamented is the Battle of Ronaldsway (Derbyhaven's original name) in 1275 when Manx forces were defeated by the Scots. The first-ever running of the Derby horserace took place near here but only Manx-bred horses were allowed to compete because the seventh Earl of Derby considered them to be the strongest and fastest.

Part of the old racecourse site is now occupied by the golf links which extends for about 3 miles (5km) and has its own hotel. Connected with the peninsula by a short causeway is St Michael's Isle with a circular fort built in 1645 and a small, ruined chapel of great antiquity.

Opposite: Walkers north of Peel on the west coast (IoM Tourism)

LANGNESS LIGHTHOUSE

From Derbyhaven to the southern point of the Langness peninsula is an invigorating walk of about 6 miles (10km) there and back, the rewards being a view of rocks contorted into arches, grottoes and pillars by the relentless action of the sea and an abundance of birds and wildflowers. In 1996 the Langness Point lighthouse became the last of five in the Island to be automated.

COASTAL AND MOUNTAIN GLENS

Manx glens are among the most captivating of all the Island's natural features. Seventeen are National Glens, maintained and preserved by the Forestry Department and, in keeping with ancient rights, no charge is made for admission. There are two types: deep wooded coastal glens with streams and waterfalls, often leading to a small, secluded beach, and mountain glens with rushing streams and miles of open moorland. Some of the streams were used to power mills of various kinds in the eighteenth and nineteenth centuries and a few have been preserved.

Glens are to be found in most parts of the Island and each has a distinctive character. Some of the best-known coastal glens are situated between Douglas and Ramsey: Dhoon, the deepest, descends steeply through fir and larch to a rocky coastline and has a 130ft (40m) waterfall in two drops; Ballaglass Glen is altogether leafier and brighter. T.E. Brown found it 'delicious in the sunlight with the beechen spray breathing over it' and full of primroses and bluebells. Old Maughold village is a 3 mile (5km) walk away and there are splendid views from Maughold Head.

On the other side of the Island, Glen Maye, with its 200ft (61m) gorge and 40ft (12m) cataract, is an extension of Glen Rushen, a deep valley running inland to South Barrule. Popular Glen Helen is named after the daughter of a Mr Marsden from Liverpool who acquired the extensive Rhenass estate and planted a million trees. There are miles of pleasant walks, a wishing seat and a waterfall not far from the entrance.

Most impressive of the mountain glens is Sulby (Great Glen) which extends for 6 miles (10km) from the source of its river on the slopes of Beinn-y-Phott, Snaefell and Sartfell to Sulby village on the edge of the lowland plain. There is just room for the river and road to descend from the rugged uplands, the bare slopes on either side becoming richly wooded 2 miles (3km) from the village. Sulby Glen and reservoir is revered by ramblers, anglers, birders, photographers and artists. There are many hidden corners such as the Cluggid Falls with a drop of 160ft (49m) in five successive leaps, reached by following a tributary stream which comes in opposite Mount Karrin. The Alt Falls plunge 30ft (9m) through a mossy, rock gorge in Tholt-y-Will, at the north-western foot of Snaefell. One of the best mountain views is from high ground above this thickly wooded mini-glen.

TRANSPORTS OF DELIGHT

'Let Isle of Man Transport chauffeur you around', say the posters. No idle boast – the Manx government has invested in an integrated system which makes travelling on public transport a positive pleasure. Special Freedom Tickets may be used freely on any combination of buses, steam railways,

Opposite: Beautiful waterfall in one of the Island's seventeen national glens

electric and mountain trams and even the horse-drawn 'toast racks' which trundle along Douglas promenade.

Just about every part of the Island can be reached by bus (public service goes before profitability) but the undoubted stars of the transport show are the charming and efficient vintage railways. To travel on any of the five Victorian lines is to step back into a gentler, less-frenetic age. A constant source of delight to passengers is to ride in the original carriages behind engines up to 120 years old, maintained in pristine condition by generations of Manx railwaymen. The government funds special workshops where skilled engineers replace working parts and restore fittings and finishes on all steam and electric rolling stock. They work from the original design drawings.

A HEAD OF STEAM

Fun and pure nostalgia is the only way to describe a trip on the Douglas to Port Erin steam railway, at 17 miles (27km) the longest 3ft (1km) narrow-gauge line in the British Isles. Puffing and rattling through gentle pastoral scenery, the little trains stop at Port Soderick, Ballasalla, Castletown, Colby and Port St Mary plus request halts along the way. At Port Erin station, the waiting rooms are full of railway memorabilia and there is a railway museum which tells the story of Manx steam.

Once part of an Island-wide steam-railway network, the Douglas-Port Erin route was established in 1874, a year after the opening of the first line (Douglas to Peel). Later services linked Peel to Ramsey and there was a line from St John's to the Foxdale mines. The increase in road traffic led to a decline in demand after the Second World War and the lines to Peel and Ramsey were closed. Some of the old tracks have become heritage trails but the Manx government did save the Douglas-Port Erin line which operates from Easter to mid-autumn.

Groudle Glen, a 2ft (0.6m) gauge steam railway, celebrated its centenary in 1996 having been restored by a team of ardent enthusiasts. The original engine 'Sea Lion' carries passengers for three-quarters of a mile (just over a kilometre) through woodland onto the cliff tops. It operates on Sundays from mid-May to mid-September, and at other times which can be checked in advance. The smallest gauge on the Island (3.5in; 9cm) is the miniature Orchid Line which operates in the Curraghs Wildlife Park, near Ballaugh.

ELECTRIC TRAMS

Manx Electric Railways (saved by the government in 1958) operates the world's oldest working tram cars over an 18-mile (29km) coastal route between Douglas and Ramsey. The first section was opened in 1893, and the entire line was completed in 1898 linking the two largest towns before the motor car became king. Acclaimed as one of the most scenic routes in these islands, the smart, single-decker trams stay close to the coastline for most of the run, riding along the clifftops and snaking inland past glens, hills and hamlets. Stops and halts include Groudle Glen, Baldrine, Ballabeg, Fairy Cottage, Dhoon Glen, Ballaglass and Ballajora (for Maughold) and finally Ramsey, where there is a visitor centre.

Roughly halfway is leafy Laxey station (for the Great Laxey Wheel and Mines Trail), where passengers can switch to the 3ft 6in (1.1m) gauge electric mountain railway and a stately 5-mile (8km) ride to the summit of Snaefell. The line was built between January and August 1895 in spite of bad weather and gradients as steep as 1 in 12. It takes half an hour to climb

HORSE-DRAWN TRAMS

Douglas has the world's oldest horse-drawn tram service, continuous since 1876 apart from wartime breaks. Countless thousands have enjoyed a leisurely trot in closed or open-sided carriages ('toast racks') along the impressive 2 mile (3km) sweep of promenade from the sea terminal to Derby Castle where the electric railway starts and finishes. There is no need to sympathise with the horses: they enjoy the exercise and the tramcars, all fitted with roller bearings, could be pulled easily, fully laden, by a single man. There are 23 tramcars and 42 horses which work for only 2 hours per day in the season and have all winter off. Specially bred and trained for the job these much-loved animals are eventually retired to a Home of Rest on the outskirts of Douglas, where they can be visited by the public.

Above: Horse-drawn tram on Douglas promenade
Opposite above: Groudle Glen has a 2ft gauge steam railway
Opposite below: Snaefell Mountain Railway was the first of its kind

up through Laxey Glen with views of the Lady Isabella wheel, river, woods and heathland. Trams stop at the Bungalow on the TT mountain course, close to the Motor Cycle Museum. At the summit there are viewing platforms, a licensed restaurant and a railway exhibition. Mist on the top is not uncommon but on a clear day the views over the Island and the surrounding countries are unequalled. The railway operates from May to September.

CYCLING TRAILS

There are six one-day cycling trails each distinctly signed with route numbers and directions. A map is available showing total distances, degrees of difficulty, major climbs and descents, and sites of interest. All, excepting the Peel trail, are accessible by steam train or MER tram. The route around Douglas is a demanding 27 miles (43km), taking in quiet country lanes, several steep hills and finishing on the Marine Drive. From Castletown the run to St Mark's is an easy 13 miles (21km) with no major climbs, passing Ballasalla (with a diversion to Silverdale Glen), Rushen Abbey and Castle Rushen. Optional add-on rides are along the coast to Derbyhaven and St Michael's Isle and the Langness peninsula. Coastal scenery, wildlife and quaint villages are attractions on the 13-mile (21km) round trip from Port Erin to Colby, Ballabeg, Balladoole burial site, and Port St Mary, with optional diversions to Cregneash (a long, steep hill to climb) and the Sound, overlooking the Calf of Man. A little easier is the 10-mile (16km) trail starting and finishing in Peel (the castle, House of Manannan etc), taking in pretty Glen Maye and St John's (Tynwald Hill, craft centre) and a climb up to 'Snuff the Wind' for wide-ranging views of the Island.

There are no stiff climbs on the 16-mile (25km) cycle trail over the quiet, flat country roads of the northern Ayres. From Ramsey MER station, the route runs along the Mooragh Promenade before gaining the road to Bride (home of Sir Norman Wisdom for many years). From Bride a diversion leads to the Point of Ayre lighthouse, the most northerly part of the Island, and where there is a visitor centre and nature trail. Back on the main trail, the road leads to the Lhen, passing Knock-e-Doonee burial site and on to Andreas (Norse stone crosses in the churchyard). After Ballachurry Civil War Fort is St Jude's and, outside Ramsey, the Grove Rural Life Museum.

The round trip from Laxey to Ballaquine, rated 'short but hard', covers only 6 miles (10km) but it involves an initial lung-bursting climb. Places of interest include Ballalheanaagh gardens, 'King Orry's Grave', Laxey Great Wheel, the Mines Trail, Fairy Cottage and the woollen mills.

Fourteenth-century Monk's Bridge, Ballasalla, lies on an old packhorse route

Opposite top: South Barrule Cringle plantation from Magnetic Hill

Opposite centre: Port St Mary

Opposite below: Norse Dragon cross-slab, Kirk Michael

Below: Wheel-headed cross-slab, Lonan – more Celtic than Norse in style

THE HIGH ROADS AND THE LOW ROADS

Private coach operators provide the traditional round-the-Island-tours, popularised by the charabanc in the first half of the last century, and there are regular morning, afternoon and evening coach trips to specific places and events. Given the cost of bringing vehicles to the Isle of Man, car hire is a useful option, especially for short visits – hire vehicles range from compact four-seaters to minibuses, with all seats belted. There is a Manx Highway Code (available from bookshops) but the majority of roadsigns will be familiar to UK motorists. There are restrictions in towns and a parking disc (easily obtainable) is essential.

DOUGLAS-LAXEY-RAMSEY

To allow for leisurely exploration, the most rewarding day tours by car rarely exceed 40 miles (64km). One of many classic excursions is from Douglas to Ramsey via Laxey on the 16 miles (26km) of the A2 coastal road, which runs close to the scenic MER tram route. Just beyond Onchan is Molly Quirk's little glen and, approaching Baldrine hamlet, there is a narrow diversion to Old Lonan Church and its ancient crosses. Back on the A2, the road reaches Garwick (Norse *Gjarvik* = 'cave creek') with its glen and deep smugglers' caves, full of contraband in the heyday of the Manx 'running trade'. Nearby are the Cloven Stones, the remains of a prehistoric burial cairn, now surrounded by houses.

Before the winding descent to Laxey village, the road follows the sweep of Laxey Bay which stretches from Clay Head to Laxey Head. There is more coastal scenery beyond Laxey as the road climbs up to Minorca near the megalithic King Orry's Grave. After deep and dark Dhoon Glen, a minor road leads to Glen Mona with access to Port Cornaa beach, Cashtal-yn-Ard burial ground and pretty Ballaglass Glen.

A right turn onto the A15 is the way to Maughold. Just before the village, a turning leads down to tiny Port Mooar, a peaceful and secluded inlet. Leaving Maughold and its celebrated Celtic crosses, ruined keeills, lighthouse and exceptional coastal scenery, the A15 provides views over the great sweep of Ramsey Bay before rejoining the A2 for the descent to Ramsey. The return to Douglas over the famous TT course (A18) might allow for a stop to admire the mountains and moors or a trip to the top of Snaefell from the Bungalow.

CASTLETOWN-PORT ST MARY-PORT ERIN

Another classic day tour is from Castletown (A5), past Balladoole to Port St Mary, continuing on the A31 to Cregneash and the Calf Sound, returning on a minor road to Port Erin. The route then follows the A32 up the slopes to Bradda onto the A36 Sloc road to the Round Table crossroads beneath South Barrule. (Back-tracking on the A27 to Ronague allows motorists to experience the optical illusion of Magnetic Hill, although folklore insists that fairies are responsible for making vehicles travel up hill when they appear to be going down.)

Back on course, Dalby and Glen Maye are soon reached. Near the post office the narrow Garey turning leads to the 'Back of the Moon' road past old mine workings before rejoining the main road to Foxdale (Norse *Fossdal* = waterfall dale – there are no foxes in the Island). The A24 past Eairy Dam and Braaid leads to the A6 and the return to Castletown via Santon, Fairy Bridge (raise your hat to the lil' people!) and Ballasalla. The old Castletown Road (A25), nearer the coast, is an alternative route.

DOUGLAS-BALDWIN VALLEY-PEEL

Douglas to Peel, via the beautiful Baldwin valley, begins with an exhilarating 8-mile (13km) run into the mountains. From Douglas, the Strang road (A23) continues to the top of Mount Rule which provides a grandstand view up the East and West Baldwin valleys. A right-hand turn onto the B22 begins a 5-mile (8km) descent to Baldwin with the River Glass below flanked by steep, wooded slopes. A minor road leads to the East Baldwin valley and St Luke's Chapel (near the site of an ancient Tynwald where a law was passed suppressing trial by combat) before rejoining the main road. Ahead lies Injebreck reservoir and extensive larch and pine plantations set in a deep mountain recess at the top of West Baldwin valley.

The road rises between Colden, 1,599ft (487m), and Carraghan, 1,640ft (500m), to emerge at Brandywell (B10), where mountain sheep were branded. The route continues along the single-track Druidale Road across open moorland with mountains, including Snaefell, on all sides, before descending through a glen to Ballaugh village and the main Ramsey-Peel road (A3). Nearby is the extensive Curraghs nature reserve and wildlife park. Heading for Peel and about a mile from Kirk Michael the road passes Bishopscourt, residence of Manx bishops for 800 years up to 1980. The 14-acre (6ha) Bishop's Glen is opposite.

Kirk Michael, a substantial village close to the sea, has the largest group of Norse crosses in the Island, preserved in the church. Five bishops are buried in the old churchyard. After Michael and Glen Wyllin (which runs down to the beach) the A4 into Peel goes by Glen Mooar with the Spooyt Vane ('white spout') waterfall and the ruins of a keeill set in trees. After Peel, the main road (A1) is taken through St John's back to Douglas.

7 THE 'LOST' INDUSTRIES

Old agricultural skills are demonstrated at Cregneash Folk Village

Near the top of Sulby Glen lie the ruins of several upland farms, some reduced to a few stones hidden among trees. Gorse and bracken have reclaimed the fields: Sharragh Vane, the setting for a narrative poem by T.E. Brown, is marked only by a white, quartz stone (the name means 'white foal'). Other farm names, such as Creg Mooar and Creggans, are largely forgotten. A little chapel and a school building have survived; sheep browse, hawks dive-bomb the moorland but the farming families are long gone.

The inevitable decline of crofting throughout the British Isles applies equally to the Isle of Man. For centuries, generations of Manx people were dependent on crofting and fishing or a combination of both and, in some parts of the Island, their way of life survived into the twentieth century. Today, a scatter of ruined farmhouses ('tholtans') and a few boats landing shellfish are the most obvious reminders of the old crofter-fisherman tradition. While agriculture continues to be very much in evidence (80 per cent of the landmass is cultivated or grazed), farming and fishing combined contribute less than 2 per cent to the Island's income. Another 'lost' industry – mining for valuable metals – was a source of considerable employment and wealth in the nineteenth century.

Manx National Heritage has thoroughly researched the social and economic aspects of Manx farming, fishing and mining. The experiences of those who depended on the old industries are brought to life by the Story of Mann presentation in Douglas, the House of Manannan in Peel, Cregneash Folk Village, Grove Rural Life Museum near Ramsey and the Great Laxey Wheel & Mines Trail. What comes through even the briefest examination of these subjects is the sheer hardiness of the people.

WASTE NOT, WANT NOT

Like the Scots, the Manx have a reputation for caution and thrift: 'Better to go to bed without supper than to rise in debt' is an old saying. For centuries, Manx crofters had little choice but to be self-sufficient. Almost everything in their immediate environment was put to good use: stones for buildings, rope made from straw ('suggane'), clothes fashioned from home-produced wool and flax, sandals made of rawhide ('carranes'); even the prolific gorse was bruised and fed to animals. Before 1800, they made their own tools and transported everything on sledges or panniers ('creels') strapped on the backs of ponies. It was endless back-breaking toil from dawn to dusk with the women doing more than their share, especially when the men were 'away at the fishin'.

Farms in the Isle of Man fell into three categories: substantial quarterland estates (sub-divisions of the ancient treens); smaller 'intacks', often in the uplands, created by the enclosures of grazing areas and common land; and the little crofts. Crofters had only a few acres and would often help out on a larger farm in exchange for a rent-free cottage. Co-operation between neighbouring farms was essential when it came to ploughing, harvesting and cutting turf for fuel. Life, as the Manx would say, was 'terrible hard', yet they raised large families and enjoyed themselves on high days and holidays. Music and dancing was a feature at fairs and weddings, and when itinerant fiddler/story-tellers visited the farms.

GONE FISHING!

Herring fishing was always a boom-and-bust business: huge catches one year, virtual failure the next. In 1765, more than 20,000 barrels of salted herring were exported from the Isle of Man but by 1835 the Manx fishing fleet had declined from more than 400 vessels to less than 200. The industry revived in the 1850s when better-equipped boats turned fishing into a year-round activity with cod and mackerel being caught in addition to herring.

HARDY, LONG-LIVED PEOPLE

John Feltham, author of A Tour of the Isle of Man, *published in 1798, remarked on the longevity of the people after inspecting tombstones in Maughold churchyard. The Manx were not exposed to the pollution and overcrowding which shortened many British lives during the industrial revolution and when they emigrated it was usually to escape an unexpected crop or herring failure. In general, the combination of mixed farming and seasonal fishing seemed to sustain the health, if not the wealth, of the people.*

Pages 94–5: Cliffs above Fleshwick Bay – Manx crofter-fishermen were never far from the sea

In the heyday of the Manx crofter-fisherman, several thousand would leave their crofts for three or four months in summer to go fishing. As George Woods observed in 1811: 'They leave their wives to turn the soil, to reap, to thresh and dig potatoes'. A decade later there are references to 'the mania for fishery which pervades all classes of the country, draining it of those who should be employed in the cultivation of the ground'.

The peak of Manx fishing was reached in the 1880s when 13,000 out of a population of 53,000 were directly or indirectly dependent on the industry. Manx harbours were packed with hundreds of local and visiting fishing boats. On the quaysides, a small army of cheery 'fishwives' (some brought in from Scotland) cleaned, salt-cured and packed the herring in barrels: the famous smoke-cured Manx kippers did not become big business until after 1900. Improvements in fishing and processing methods attracted a growing number of Scottish, Irish and other 'foreign' vessels and the Manx fleet was unable to compete. Many fishing families turned to the new industry – tourism.

Impressive catches continued to be made from the Manx fishing grounds (25,000 tonnes in 1974) but activity has been curbed by conservation measures. An international demand for Queen scallops (once used as bait) arrived in the 1970s and Manx fishermen were quick to exploit shellfish beds in local waters. Scallops and queenies now account for more than 90 per cent of the value of seafood landed in the Isle of Man and most landings are by Manx vessels. These delicacies are widely exported and are also part of the Island's cuisine along with fresh fish, lobsters, Manx lamb, kippers and bonnag.

Mining Valuable Metals

Now a major tourist attraction 'Lady Isabella', the Great Laxey Wheel, was once a part of the prolific Manx mining industry. A good deal of enterprise and sweat characterised the production of huge quantitites of lead, zinc, copper, silver and iron ore during the nineteenth century. The industry developed rapidly after 1830 and peaked between 1850 and 1890, providing much-needed jobs and good returns for investors. In 1871, 1,444 people were employed above and below ground mainly at Foxdale and Laxey, and at some 40 smaller mines and 80 mining trails. Experienced miners came from Cornwall, Scotland and other parts of the UK to supplement the local workforce.

From today's comparatively enlightened standpoint the men worked in appalling conditions, although Manx mines were no worse than those in other countries. There were fatal accidents: in May 1897, 20 men died from carbon-monoxide poisoning at Snaefell mine leaving 11 widows and 30 fatherless children. Other accidents resulted from flooding which is why the giant Laxey wheel was so important: 'Lady Isabella' was capable of raising 250 gallons (1,137 litres) of water per minute from a depth of 200 fathoms (365m).

Mining for metal in the Isle of Man began in the Bronze Age (local copper was mixed with imported tin to produce bronze) and continued through every phase of Manx history with mixed success until rich seams of valuable ore were found. Laxey became the leading supplier of zinc in the British Isles, in addition to producing lead ore rich in silver, and Foxdale was a major source of lead until the ore was exhausted and world markets changed. The industry gradually dwindled and the last mine closed in 1929.

Arches at Laxey Wheel – an elegant legacy from a grimy past

8 THRILLS, SPILLS AND GENTLER PURSUITS

THE TT RACES

Even the briefest look at Sporting Mann has to begin with the famous Tourist Trophy motorcycle races and other events which have earned for the Isle of Man the title of 'Road Racing Capital of the World'. For several weeks each summer this peaceful island is invaded by more than 50,000 bikers from all over Europe and beyond. They gather, mainly in Douglas, to celebrate the TT Festival which starts in late May.

Apart from comparing motorcyles, indulging in endless biker chat and enjoying reunions with old friends, these colourful enthusiasts come to watch professional riders lapping the hair-raising TT course at around 125mph (200kph), and reaching speeds up to 180mph (290kph). There is no more challenging test of man and machine than the 37.73 miles (61km) circuit which corkscrews between stone walls, hedges and houses and hurtles over the Snaefell mountain road.

When the roads are not closed for racing or practice (early mornings and evenings), thousands of visiting and resident bikers buzz around the TT course. A few try too hard to emulate the professionals and every year there are accidents, some fatal. Race riders have also paid the ultimate price for mechanical failure, a split-second loss of concentration or a patch of oil on the road. Risks are weighed against the desire to compete in the greatest sporting challenge of its kind in the world, and banning the TT would be like preventing attempts on Everest.

Involvement in road racing goes back to Tynwald's Road Closure Act (1904) which enabled British entries to try out for the Gordon Bennett Cup competition due to be held in France. The object was to assess the reliability and speed of touring cars and to encourage their development.

When the trials ended in 1905, Tourist Trophy car races were run over the same course: Douglas to Castletown, Peel, Ramsey and back to Douglas over the mountain road. TT motorcycle races began in 1907 over a shorter course, moving in 1911 to the circuit we know today. Early riders often had to dismount and push their belt-driven iron steeds and, on occasion, open and close gates! Fifty miles per hour (80kph) was really motoring in those days. Improved machines and road surfaces soon made for an increasingly thrilling spectacle and 100mph (160kph) lap-times were in sight by the end of the 1930s.

The TT became the blue riband of motorcycling, attracting huge crowds and the cream of international riders. Every generation has had its

Fast and furious – the TT is the most challenging of all motorcycle events (IoM Tourism)

BIKERS' BLISS

Other motorcycle events include the three-day Southern 100 on the Billown road-race circuit, the Manx Grand Prix for amateur riders over the TT course (September), pre-TT classic road races, the Ramsey sprint and off-road trials, motor cross and sand racing. Still on two wheels but quieter, is the International Cycling Festival held in June. TT car races transferred to Northern Ireland in 1922, but in the 1930s Douglas staged 'round the houses' races and, after the war, the British Empire Trophy.

Sailing on the lake in Mooragh Park, Ramsey (IoM Tourism)

heroes: Stanley Woods, Jimmy Guthrie, Geoff Duke, Mike Hailwood and Joey Dunlop. There are races for various categories of machine, ranging from ultra-lightweight to senior. To win is glorious but even to finish is an achievement.

Spectators gather all round the course at locations which have become part of road-racing history: Bray Hill, Quarter Bridge, Ballacraine, Laurel Bank, Baaregarrow, Ballaugh Bridge, Quarry Bends, Sulby Straight, Ramsey Hairpin, Gooseneck, the Verandah, 32nd Milestone, Windy Corner, Kate's Cottage, Creg-ny-Baa, Hillberry, Signpost, Governor's Bridge. The adrenalin flows both on and off the course and it all adds up to an exciting festival fortnight.

The Island continues to host outstanding four-wheel events: classic-car trials, national and international rallies (with some of the most testing stages in the British Isles) and kart-racing Grand Prix where karts dash through the narrow streets of Peel at up to 100mph (160kph).

SPORT UNLIMITED

The Isle of Man has another claim to sporting fame which goes back a lot further than the high-octane TT. On 28 July 1627 the Earl of Derby, Lord of Mann, inaugurated a horse race which he named after himself. It was

run on the Langness peninsula in an area still known as 'the racecourse'. In 1779 the Derby transferred to Epsom where it became the premier classic in the flat-racing calendar. Horse racing continued at the Strang and later Belle Vue, Douglas, until 1931, but today's equine favourites are engaged in show jumping and pony trekking.

Given the size and population of the Island, the range of sports and outdoor activities is exceptional. Provision is made for almost every conceivable speciality and there is professional advice on hand for those who want it. There is no shortage of spectator sport but residents are also enthusiastic participators who are only too pleased when visitors join in. Those who enjoy a challenge may opt for abseiling, rockclimbing, windsurfing or scuba diving; others might prefer a gentle swim, a round of golf, a game of tennis, a peaceful day's fishing or a visit to a sheepdog trial or a bowls festival.

WATER, WATER, EVERYWHERE

Because the Island is much narrower than it is long, nowhere (not even the highest moorland or the deepest glen) is further than 6 miles (10km) from the sea. This explains why the old crofters had little difficulty in combining farming with fishing. The sea has always been a focus of Manx life and the superb coastline of almost 100 miles (160km) is ideal for sailing, fishing and seasports. There are excellent beaches and numerous quiet inlets although, away from the established resorts, it is necessary to keep a weather eye on tides and currents. There are miles of sands and picturesque harbours at Douglas, Port Erin, Port St Mary, Ramsey, Castletown and Peel.

The Isle of Man is a busy staging post for visiting yachts (and other vessels) from all over the Irish Sea and beyond. Douglas, Peel, Ramsey and Port St Mary are the four main harbours but there is also good anchorage at Castletown, Derbyhaven, Port Erin and Laxey. A variety of sailing is available to both experienced sailors and novices. There are six sailing clubs and plenty of craft for hire, self-sail or crewed. Major maritime events include Round the Island yacht races, the Peel Festival of the Sea (traditional boats and tall ships) and Viking longship races, also at Peel. Events are held for all manner of craft ranging from dinghy trials to the world tin-bath championship in Castletown's inner harbour! Boat trips can be booked to see basking sharks, to visit the Calf of Man nature reserve, to go wreck and reef fishing or simply to explore the coastline.

The energetic engage in jet skiing, windsurfing, sand-racing and canoeing or take instruction in powerboat handling. Scuba diving in the clear waters which surround the Isle of Man can be spectacular especially in the south where there is such a diversity of marine life. Most of the many wrecks around the coast are protected but some can be dived if permission is sought.

A list of fishing locations is available from tourism offices where there is information on all activities. There is excellent sea fishing around the coast from the long surf beaches of the north to the rocky clifftops of the south. From harbour breakwaters and piers, for example, coalfish, plaice, flounder, dabs, wrasse, conger and pollack are taken and there is usually a good run of tope during Ramsey Angling Festival. Inshore reefs around Port St Mary and the Calf of Man are fished from both charter and small craft during the annual Boat Fishing Festival. Deep-sea fishing is no longer a staple industry but locally caught cod is sold in fish-and-chip shops and restaurants serve succulent scallops – known as queenies – lobsters and other fresh Manx seafood.

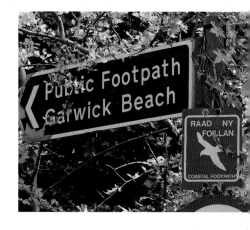

STILL WATERS AND LIVELY RIVERS

Above: Signposts are often in both Manx and English

Opposite: Manx harbours offer good shelter for yachts and larger vessels

Pages 104–5: High moorland near Snaefell and Sulby reservoir

Freshwater fishing is equally popular and there are plenty of sizeable fish to be caught – trout over 16lb (7kg) and salmon over 17lb (8kg) have been taken. Eight still-water reservoirs may be fished until the end of October and there is sport in eleven rivers and streams until the end of September. All locations are stocked with sizeable rainbow and wild brown trout, raised at the Hatchery at Ballaglass (visitors welcome).

One licence covers all eight water-authority reservoirs and a separate licence permits fishing elsewhere. Inexpensive licences, available from government and post offices, are necessary because reservoir and river watchers have powers of confiscation and arrest! On the other hand, these worthies are most helpful to the law-abiding and will advise on the best places to fish.

Most of the reservoirs are in idyllic country settings: Ballure in the hills just south of Ramsey; Block Eary, west of Sulby valley; Eairy Dam, east of Foxdale; Clypse and Kerrowdhoo, both north of Onchan; Cringle in the south; West Baldwin, a popular beauty spot, and Sulby reservoir in a spacious upland setting. Manx rivers and streams favour more intimate fishing with fly, worm or spinner. Most are stocked with brown trout, and salmon and sea trout are taken in the main streams in summer and autumn. As elsewhere, the number of migratory fish has diminished although large specimens are still being caught.

Sulby river is the longest stretch of running water, starting at the reservoir in the mountains and running down the broad glen into the sea at Ramsey. It begins as a rocky, fast-flowing stream tumbling into pools and gradually widening into a deeper, slower, lowland river. Entirely different in character is the Cornaa river which rises just below North Barrule and enters the sea at Port Cornaa. There are interesting pools at Ballaglass Glen and a deep pool half a mile from the sea which is good for migratory fish.

Other rivers in the angling notebook are the Laxey, Glass, Baldwin, Santon, Silverburn, Colby, Neb and Glen Maye. A few stretches are

restricted but, in general, landowners are most accommodating, provided anglers are considerate. Some streams flow through the lovely Manx National Glens which are open to everyone.

A GOLFING PARADISE

Golf has been played in the Isle of Man for more than a hundred years. A round or two here is definitely not 'a long walk spoiled' because each of the eight courses (seven 18-hole, one 9-hole) is surrounded by superb scenery. In comparison with the UK, Manx golf courses are uncrowded and no one is more than fifty minutes by car from any other. Some courses have their own luxury hotels, facilities are excellent everywhere and visitors receive a warm Manx welcome.

Thanks to the equable climate, golf is virtually a year-round activity and packaged golf holidays are popular. Each course has a distinctive character: Castletown, for example, is a challenging links course where PGA classics have been played, while the course at Ramsey undulates through wooded parkland but is equally testing. Good golfing can be had near Douglas, at Pulrose 'pay and play' course, King Edward's Bay, Onchan, noted for its springy mountain turf and Mount Murray which measures 6,664yd (6,094m) off the back tee. Peel golf course is full of natural hazards, Rowany at Port Erin is a tough heathland course and the neat 9-holer at Port St Mary was designed by former British Open champion, George Duncan.

THE NATIONAL SPORTS CENTRE

Manx athletes and swimmers are good enough to compete in the Commonwealth Games and other major sporting events. They benefit from the all-weather facilities available at the Island's National Sports Centre in Douglas where a £10m 'state of the art' swimming pool complex was added in 1998. There are facilities for indoor and outdoor activities in most parts of the island and various venues are involved in the annual Student Festival of Sport. Track and road athletic meetings, including marathons and half-marathons, are regularly staged and an international hockey festival also features in the long list of sporting events. Cammag, a form of hockey related to the Scottish shinty, was once the Manx national sport. Rugby and cricket are played but soccer has been a passion for a hundred years with teams from every town and village competing fiercely for league championships and cups.

Golfing near Douglas – there are eight courses on the Island

FURTHER INFORMATION

TRAVEL TO THE ISLE OF MAN

Many holiday packages are inclusive of travel costs and arrangements. Air travel to the Isle of Man has never been easier. Ronaldsway airport serves fourteen destinations in England, Scotland, Wales and Ireland: Birmingham, Belfast, Blackpool, Bristol, Cardiff, Dublin, Glasgow, Jersey, Leeds-Bradford, Liverpool, London Heathrow, Luton, Manchester and Southampton. The main carrier is Manx Airlines which operates a fleet of modern aircraft including British Aerospace 146, ATP and Jetstream 41 and Embraer RJ145 regional jet. Typical flight times are: Liverpool (35min), Glasgow (50min), Birmingham (55min), London Heathrow (70min).

For those who enjoy a bracing sea crossing and/or wish to take their own cars, year-round passenger- and car-ferry services are operated from Liverpool and Heysham by the Isle of Man Steam Packet Company. In addition, there are daily sailings from Liverpool by high-speed SuperSeaCat and SeaCat and seasonal services from Belfast and Dublin. The flagship Ro-Pax ferry *Ben-my-Chree*, custom-built at a cost of £24 million, has first class facilities including *en suite* cabins. Average crossing times: Liverpool-Douglas: conventional ferry 4hr, fastcraft 2hr 30min; Heysham-Douglas: conventional ferry 3hr 30min, fastcraft 2hr; Belfast-Douglas: fastcraft 2hr 45min; Dublin-Douglas: conventional ferry 4hr 45min, fastcraft 2hr 45min.

CARAVANS AND CAMPING

Trailer caravans are not permitted on the Isle of Man. Motor caravans and tenting campers are welcome (list of registered campsites available from Tourist Information Centres).

USEFUL TELEPHONE NUMBERS

(When dialling from the UK the prefix is 01624)

Basking Shark Society	801207
Bus information line	662525
Harbour contacts:	
Douglas	686627
Laxey	861663
Peel	842338
Port St Mary, Port Erin & Castletown	833206
Ramsey	812245
Heritage information line (Manx Museum)	648000
Isle of Man (Ronaldsway) Airport	821600
Isle of Man Steam Packet Company	661661
Laxey Heritage Trust (summer only)	862007
Manx Airlines (Central Reservations)	824313
Manx Bird Atlas	861130
Manx Ornithological Society	824395
Manx Wildlife Trust	801985
National Sports Centre	688588
Railways information line	663366
Tourism & Leisure Information	
Douglas	686766
fax:	627443
Sea Terminal Buildings,	
Douglas, IoM, 1M1 2RG	
web site: http//www.gov.im/tourism;	
e-mail address: tourism @ gov.im	
Other Information Offices (open all year)	
Castletown	825005
Onchan	621228
Peel	842341
Port Erin	832298/835858
Port St Mary	832101
Ramsey	817025
Weather Check	888300

MANX PLACE NAMES AND THEIR MEANINGS

Place names in the Isle of Man are predominantly Gaelic: some 18 per cent are of Norse origin.

Gaelic components include:

ard	height
balla	farm, place
beg, veg	little
broogh	bank, brow
cashtal	castle, earthwork
claddagh	river meadow
creg	rock
croit	croft
cronk, crink	hill
curragh	marsh, bog
drine	thorn tree
garroo	rough
glion	glen
gob	point, promontory
keeill	chapel, church
knock	hillock
lag, laggan	hollow, ditch
logh	lake
moddee	dog
mooar, vooar	great
pooyl	pool
purt	harbour
reeast	moorland
sallagh	willow
slieau	mountain
spooyt	waterfall
tramman	elder tree
ushag	bird

Examples of Manx Gaelic place names:

Baldrine	place of the black thorn
Ballachrink	hill farm
Ballasalla	village of the willow river
Ballaugh	homestead of the lake
Cashtal yn Ard	castle of the height
Creg-ny-Baa	rock of the cow
Croit ny Ushag	croft of the bird
Cronk y Voddee	hill of the dog
Gliontramman	glen of the elder trees
Gob ny Roinna	point of the seal
Kerroomoar	great quarterland
Lag ny Keilley	hollow of the church
Slieau Ruy	red mountain

Norse components include:

aa	river
by	homestead
dal	vale
foss	waterfall
gardr	garth, farm
howe	hill
kirkja	church
lang	long
nes	headland
sandr	sand
thing	assembly
vik	creek

Examples of Norse place names:

Dalby	dale settlement
Dyrabyr, Jurby	gravelly bank farm
Fiskgadr, Fistard	fish farm
Forsdalr, Foxdale	waterfall dale
Langness	long peninsula
Perwick	Peter's creek
Sartfell	black mountain

FURTHER READING

Numerous Manx-interest books are available from bookshops in the towns. A considerable bibliography of the Isle of Man can be accessed at the Manx Museum in Douglas. A wide selection of books, leaflets and maps is available from Tourism & Leisure Information Offices, and from Manx National Heritage – see useful telephone numbers. *Inheritance* (see below) includes a comprehensive list of titles. Available from 21 Spring Valley, Douglas, Isle of Man IM2 4EU.

Bazin, F.C. *Ree ny Marrey: Songs of the Isle of Man* (Manx Heritage Foundation, 1994)

—, — . *Much Inclin'd to Music* (Manx Heritage Foundation, 1997)

Cottle, Valerie (ed). *Inheritance – the Living Culture of Mann* (Manx Heritage Foundation and Executive Publications) Published twice yearly.

Craine, David. *Manannan's Isle* (Manx Museum, 1995)

Cubbon, A.M. *The Ancient & Historic Monuments of the Isle of Man* (Manx National Heritage, revised edition 1994)

—, — . *Prehistoric Sites in the Isle of Man* (Manx National Heritage, revised edition 1995)

—, — . *The Art of Manx Crosses* (Manx National Heritage, revised edition 1996)

Garrad, Larch S. *The Naturalist in the Isle of Man* (David & Charles, 1972)

Kelly, Alan (ed/art consultant). *The Art of Mann* (Moods of Mann Ltd, 1996)

Kinvig, R.H. *The Isle of Man: a Social, Cultural & Political History* (Liverpool University Press, 1975)

Kneale, P. *Ninety Years of TT Magic* (Manx Experience, 1998)

Kniveton, G.N. (ed). *An Illustrated Encyclopedia of the Isle of Man* (The Manx Experience, 1997)

Manx Heritage Foundation (information packs)
Manx Farming & Country Life: 1700-1900 (1991)
Manx Sea Fishing (1991)
Manx Mines, Rocks & Minerals (1994)

Moore, A.W. *History of the Isle of Man*, 2 vols (Manx National Heritage, reprinted 1992)

Moore, A.W. *Folklore of the Isle of Man*, 1891 (republished SR Publishing, 1971)

Quayle, George E. *Legends of a Lifetime* (Douglas Printers, 1979)

Quilliam, Leslie. *Surnames of the Manks* (Cashtal Books, 1989)

ACKNOWLEDGEMENTS

The following gave invaluable help in the preparation of this book:
Victor Kneale CBE MA(hc); Anna Hemy, IoM Tourism & Leisure; Caroline Steel and Cathy Pridham, Manx Wildlife Trust; Dr Andrew Foxon, Manx National Heritage; Chris Sharpe, Manx Bird Atlas; Alan Kelly, Mannin Collections Ltd; Ken Watterson, Basking Shark Society; Dr Fenella Bazin, Centre for Manx Studies; Roger Sims, Archivist, Manx Museum, and his staff; Miles Cowsill, Lily Publications (IoM) Ltd; Alfred Gatfield.
(Where appropriate, the use of photographs and map references is gratefully acknowledged.)

INDEX

Page numbers in *italics* indicate illustrations